MERSEYSIDE

THE INDIAN SUMMER

Volume 2
Return to Pier Head

Wallasey • Liverpool • The Hinterland

CEDRIC GREENWOOD

·THE HERITAGE OF BRITAIN·
from
The NOSTALGIA Collection

First published in 2007

British Library Cataloguing in Publication Data

A catalogue record for this book is available from the British Library.

ISBN 978 1 85794 273 6

Silver Link Publishing Ltd
The Trundle
Ringstead Road
Great Addington
Kettering
Northants NN14 4BW

Tel/Fax: 01536 330588
email: sales@nostalgiacollection.com
Website: www.nostalgiacollection.com

Printed and bound in the Czech Republic

All photographs and drawings are by the author unless otherwise credited.

Front cover picture The impressive trinity of the Liver, Cunard and Dock Buildings on George's Pier Head, flanked by the Pacific Building and warehouses on the dock road, are seen in this view of Liverpool waterfront from the Woodside ferry in 1961. The Royal Liver Building (left, 1908-11) was the head office of the Royal Liver Friendly Society, Canadian Pacific, 11 other steamship lines and the district tax offices. The Cunard Building (centre, 1914-16) was head office of the Cunard, White Star Line, eight other shipping lines and the American consulate. The Dock Building (right, 1903-07) was the home of the Mersey Docks & Harbour Board, whose survey, salvage and fire-fighting vessel *Salvor*, of 1947, is berthed at the south end of the landing stage. The Pacific Building (far right, 1896-98) was built for the White Star Line, which merged with Cunard in 1934. It was now the office of the Pacific Steam Navigation Company.

Back cover picture The parades of shops on Wallasey Road, Wallasey, photographed in 1963 (see page 65). *Both Cedric Greenwood*

CONTENTS

Left The roundabout at **SEAVIEW ROAD, LISCARD**, was the hub of the road system in Wallasey. A corporation gardener is planting a new floral display and mowing the grass bank around it. The Capitol Cinema stands on the corner of Seaview Road (left) and Liscard Village (the old village street, off to the right) and has a side entrance with a glass canopy in Seaview Road. This cinema occupies one of three sites considered in 1912 for Wallasey Town Hall, which was eventually built on North Mead, Seacombe, dominating the riverfront. This site, known as Gibbons Corner, was then occupied by stables. The 1,390-seat cinema and the adjoining parades of shops opened in 1926. Under the curved cast-iron and glass canopy on the street corner the Capitol shared its frontage with Barclay's Bank (right) and Tuckshops (confectioners, left). The cinema construction in 1926 transformed the centre of Liscard, being flanked by parades of shops integral with the cinema building:

11 shops up Seaview Road (eight of them seen here with their canvas sun canopies extended) and three more fronting on to Liscard Village. The Capitol was one of 12 cinemas in Wallasey in the 1950s (all now closed). At the time of this 1948 photograph it was screening the psychiatrist drama *Mine Own Executioner*, with Burgess Meredith and Kieron Moore, released in 1947. The cinema was modernised in 1959 but closed in 1974 (the existing building survives as a bingo hall). There was another cinema a little way up Seaview Road, on the left – the Liscard Palace (1911 to 1959). The tarred-over tram tracks up the middle of Seaview Road, disused since 1933, were lifted in 1951. The Wellington Hotel (left) was built in 1937 on the corner of Wallasey Road. Both the Capitol Cinema and the Wellington Hotel are built in the simplified classical revival style of the inter-war period. *Valentine's postcard*

ACKNOWLEDGEMENTS

My thanks go to Steve Howe of The Black & White Picture Place, Hoole, Chester, and to Glynn Parry of Bromborough for their care in coaxing the best out of my box camera photographs of 1950-61. The photographs I took from 1961 onward are copied direct from my transparencies.

I have supplemented my own photographs with selected picture postcards I bought on Merseyside in the 1950s. Many of these pictures were published by Valentine & Sons of Dundee and I thank St Andrews University Library, which holds the major archive of Valentine's monochrome topographical views, for permission to reproduce the Valentine's postcards in this book and for providing me with the dates. I also thank The Francis Frith Collection of Teffont, Wiltshire, Judges Postcards Ltd of Hastings and The Salmon Studio of Sevenoaks for permission to use the copyright on their postcards. Many of the other postcard publishers are now extinct and I cannot trace any copyright holders and many picture postcards reproduced here are anonymous. Pages from the Liverpool and New Brighton guide books of 1949-50 are reproduced by permission of Wirral Borough Council and Liverpool City Council. All the postcards and guide books I have used here are from my own collection.

In writing the text I have often referred to the following local residents, who have cheerfully shared their specialist knowledge: the late Jack Barlow of West Kirby; Jack Gahan of Fairfield, Liverpool; Joyce Hockey of New Brighton; Martin Jenkins of Walton-on-Thames; Bruce Maund of Oxton; Glynn Parry of Bromborough; and Tom Turner of Upper Brighton. I am indebted to the reference library staff of the Birkenhead and Wallasey Central Libraries for patiently plying me with old street directories and maps and posting me photocopies of entries in the directories I had overlooked. I am also indebted to the staff of Wirral Archives at Birkenhead Town Hall, Merseyside Maritime Museum archives and library at Liverpool, Crosby reference library and the Office for National Statistics at Newport (Mon). I should also single out the following officers who have supplied me with literature or given their time to answer my questions: Eric Leatherbarrow (corporate affairs officer) of the Mersey Docks & Harbour Company; Brian Wright (operations manager) and Roger Thomas (commercial manager) of Garston docks for Associated British Ports; Gerald Dickinson of the Manchester Ship Canal Company (marketing and administration) at Runcorn docks; Catherine Elwyn (Mersey estuary development coordinator) of the Mersey Basin Campaign and Mersey Waterfront; Lawson Little (membership secretary and sales officer) of the Narrow Gauge Railway Society; Peter Kennerley (former education officer) at St James's Cathedral, Liverpool; Jo-Anne Colby of Canadian Pacific Railway Archives, Montreal; Sue Newell (head of education) at the Empire Theatre, Liverpool; Colin Bell (head of the applications group) of the Proudman Oceanographic Laboratory at the former Bidston Observatory; and Tony Thomas (records officer) of the Sentinel Drivers' Club.

INTRODUCTION

The year is 1950. We are taking the keen, salty air – and the odd whiff of smoke, steam and cylinder oil – on the wide, open foredeck of a Wallasey Corporation ferry steamer as it ploughs its passage across the choppy Mersey towards its home borough. We are in transition from Volume 1 to Volume 2 of a perambulation through Merseyside in the post-war heyday of the port of Liverpool and the seaside resort of New Brighton in the Indian summer of the Industrial Age and the old order of civilisation.

It was a scene of great animation and interest, very different from the run-down and mutilated urban desert we see today. Merseyside has changed radically in the 50 years since these photographs were taken. Physically it has changed more than 50 per cent, while its character, atmosphere and social scene has changed 100 per cent, so that nobody visiting Merseyside today could imagine it only half a century ago.

In 1949-52 Merseyside was my home. Then, as an exile, for the rest of the 1950s and the early '60s it was a place of pilgrimage for me. The metamorphosis of Merseyside in the context of evolution and the decline of Great Britain has been so complete that today, only 50 years later, it hurts too much to go back. I should have taken my leave of Merseyside in the late 1950s because I prefer to remember it as it is in the photographs of that decade. This was the real Merseyside.

In the Prologue to this work in Volume 1 I described the decline of Merseyside from the closure of the Liverpool Overhead Railway in 1956 down to the closure of New Brighton Ferry in 1971, the last liner from Liverpool in 1972 and the nadir of the residual freight trade in the docks in 1984. I explained why I have used 'then and before' comparison pictures rather than 'then and now' contrasts. People who live here know what it is like today but, for the record and for those not familiar with Merseyside today, I summarised the main scene changes in Birkenhead and its dockland and on the Mersey ferries. Now let me take you through the main scene changes in Wallasey, Liverpool and the hinterland since these pictures were taken.

The residential and shopping areas in the southern half of Wallasey island have gone to seed. The railway through Poulton to Seacombe closed in 1963 and its rock gorge has been blasted out and usurped by the constant roar of traffic on the approach to the new Wallasey road tunnel under the Mersey, built in 1966-74 (the first bore opened to traffic in 1971). The tunnel ventilation station at Seacombe is a sensationally ugly concrete landmark on the Mersey promenade; contrast this with George's Dock Ventilation Station of 1934 on the Birkenhead road tunnel in Liverpool, now one of the city's architectural gems. The curved, red-sandstone Midland Bank at Seacombe crossroads degenerated to a night club and has been demolished. The floral roundabout in the centre of Liscard has gone and one-way traffic circumnavigates an anonymous 1960s shopping 'precinct' and new offices in concrete and grim, black brick. Why black brick?

The northern half of the island – northern Egremont, Upper Brighton, New Brighton and Wallasey – has remained relatively unspoiled, but closed shops, poorly maintained roads, unsympathetic new street furniture, the excess of poles, roadsigns and railings, the clutter of parked cars that reduces streets to single-line traffic flow, neglect of individual houses and gardens and the odd house 'improvements' that spoil the neat uniformity of the neighbourhood – all these factors detract from the general amenity of these areas too.

New Brighton is the classic ghost seaside resort. It has lost its ferry and two piers, its Tower and the ballroom, theatre, fairground, athletics ground and football team on the Tower campus, the Tivoli Theatre, half the shops on the main street, the three cinemas, the bathing pool, the Grand Hotel and the Hotel Victoria. Even the sands by the pier had disappeared by 1970, denuding the bedrock, and boulders are piled against the promenade wall to save it from being undermined by the sea. The sand has been won back, but only at the cost of ugly breakwaters. An even uglier pumping station marks the site of the old pier entrance. The Edwardian seafront landmark, the Avondale Café, has gone and the Royal Ferry Hotel, which appeared derelict during a hiatus as a night club, has been renovated as flats.

New Brighton has lost so much, yet it retains so much. It has lost its holiday trade and reverted to a residential town, as originally conceived. It is still a very pleasant town to live in and retains its Floral Pavilion Theatre, Art Deco-style covered amusement park, Marine Park, Vale Park and Marine Lake. The children's toy yacht pond now draws scale-model shipbuilders from a 50-mile radius, the sandy beaches have recovered, the bathing water has been cleansed by a ban on raw sewage and industrial waste in the Mersey, and residual shipping to Liverpool's north docks still gives New Brighton an interesting maritime scene.

Modern 'improvements' and developments continue to detract from the congenial environment created by our forefathers. The wide bell-mouth of Victoria Road is blocked with clutter. An excess of black railings has turned the pleasant spaciousness of Marine Promenade into the semblance of a cattle market. New Brighton has been the subject of ambitious redevelopment schemes over the past 40 years, but all have foundered on funding and feasibility. Residents had to raise £40,000 to protect their environment and fight a recent scheme for a supermarket and five-storey flats on the site of Marine Lake seaward of the promenade! The scheme had the full backing of the borough council, which purports to represent the ratepayers. It was rejected on appeal after a month-long inquiry in 2006 on account of its scale, mass and design and because it blocked the view of the fort and lighthouse and was out of character with New Brighton. But the developers will be back.

At Wallasey an isolated huddle of new brick boxes, more than 300 yards from the rest of the built-up area, has been erected on land seaward of the railway to New Brighton. This was part of the land given to the borough by the Harrison family and designated as part of Harrison Park. The obtrusive siting of these cubist flats and the better-designed houses adjacent to them detract from that glorious wide open space of grass-covered dunes and lawns that forms a buffer between the built-up area and the Irish Sea, which seems contrary to good town planning principles. Such is the municipal philistinism of modern times that the potential of the district to be a pleasant place to live is being squandered.

The Wirral motorway slices through the middle of the peninsula to tangles of concrete viaducts between Upton and Wallasey, feeding the new industrial estates, retail warehouses, tower blocks of flats and the mass of housing estates that have urbanised the country between Birkenhead, Woodchurch and Leasowe. The rural peace of South Road, Noctorum, and Townfield Lane, Oxton, has been lost in a maze of bungalows. A comparison of the Ordnance Survey maps of 1947 and 2003 shows the alarming rate at which our precious peninsula is being covered by suburban sprawl. In our post-war period, Wirral was mainly rural – now it is mainly urban.

A white, rectangular building on top of Bidston Hill, erected in 1975 as an oceanographic laboratory, is now disused, a conspicuous blot on the landscape. After 56 years as a railwaymen's convalescent home, Leasowe Castle has continued its previously chequered history with spells as an empty building, a municipal document store and now, for the third time in its history, as a hotel. Rock Channel, once the main approach to the port of Liverpool and still used by lesser vessels in the 1950s, has silted up and all ships use Crosby Channel.

As we sail up the Mersey we find that many old, familiar landmarks are missing on both sides of the river. Liverpool has been mutilated almost beyond recognition and redemption. The satanic smokestacks of dockland have gone and stacks of architectural trash in khaki, black and silver overlook the Pier Head trinity. The city is in a constant state of reconstruction. In another 50 years we shall recognise it only by its listed buildings – if they survive the mania of demolition and reconstruction for which Liverpool has been known throughout its history. Many a fine listed office building of the late 19th or early 20th century is now only partly occupied, to let as flats, or stands empty and sadly neglected, contributing to the image of ghost-town Merseyside. New buildings of the 1960s on the bombed sites of the Second World War are now among the eyesores of the city centre. A geometric glass facade intrudes into Dale Street conservation area opposite the

Town Hall. Main streets and squares have been blocked up, creating a convoluted one-way traffic system. Many acres of the inner city and dockland are urban desert with stark, modern industrial and retail sheds. And there is not a bus to be seen on Pier Head.

The 1990s brought more sensitive architecture but it is in a universal idiom and the townscape and skyline of Merseyside is losing its local identity. Conservation is winning the battle against decay of the Regency area of Liverpool and it is good to see the mature park that has replaced the threadbare football pitch in Falkner Square and the semi-rural ridge of Everton, cleared of its grim terraces and 1960s prison-like, multi-storey flats.

Along the waterfront, 4 miles of the old central and southern docks have closed. Some of the architectural, colonnaded warehouses at Albert, Wapping and Waterloo Docks have been saved and restored, but it is hard to imagine the world of the docker and stevedore, toil and grime, draught horse and steam lorry and the rumble of the Overhead in this sterilised urban desert of dereliction, car parks, luxury flats, yacht marinas, tourist shops, restaurants, offices, hotels, empty sheets of water and modern industrial estates. The Maritime Museum, which occupies Albert Dock, Canning Dock and the warehouse in between, vainly tries to recapture something of what has been lost.

The last 3 miles of docks down-river, from Nelson Dock to Seaforth Dock (opened in 1971), are still in use. The port of Liverpool was close to closure in 1984, but its fortunes have been revived by the new Mersey Docks & Harbour Company (est 1971) with massive investment in fully mechanised handling of containerised and bulk cargoes and new railway connections at Bootle, bulk cargoes at Birkenhead and duty-free transhipment zones on both sides of the river. A much reduced labour force has accepted new working practices. About 15 trains a day serve Alexandra, Gladstone and Seaforth Docks with containers, coal, steel and scrap. All grain is delivered to three new mills at Seaforth Dock. The port is now handling a greater tonnage of cargoes than ever before: 33¾ million tons in 2005, mainly imports of coal, grain, granite, oil, steel and timber, balanced by exports of scrap metal, animal feed,

chemicals, edible oils, manufactures and general cargoes. Passenger traffic is returning to the Mersey on cruise liners and Irish Sea ferries, and Liverpool Landing Stage might be re-extended to berth liners again.

This is not to say that the port is busier than ever, but things are looking up. The greater tonnage is in inverse proportion to the number of ships and the mileage of active quays because container ships and bulk carriers are larger, and fully mechanised handling allows quicker turn-round times. The port was busier in the late 19th century, when the docks were a forest of masts of smaller sailing ships and steamships berthed abreast and all goods were manhandled in barrels, boxes, bundles and sacks, but congestion and delays were chronic and the through-put of cargoes was limited. As ships have grown since the 19th century and the docks have been extended, fewer ships are needed to carry the tonnage, the docks have become less congested and the smaller docks have been abandoned.

The weight of cargo is not the sole measure of business. If we consider the volume and value of cargoes, the old staple imports such as cotton, livestock, tea, tobacco and wool, the passenger traffic on the ocean liners and troopships and the tonnage of shipping, business in the port peaked around 1900 – then two world wars and the inter-war recession culminated in a second heyday in the ten years after the Second World War, when coal, grain and iron-ore were mechanically loaded and unloaded in bulk with elevators and chutes.

Such has been the economic change since the end of the industrial age in Britain that coal and steel, once staple exports of Birkenhead and Liverpool, are now staple imports. Our largest export by volume is scrap metal to foreign steelworks. Most of the ship-owners and many of the marine services in the Mersey docks now have foreign names.

Today's ships are angular monsters with cliff-like deckhouses, lacking the glamour of the handsome sail and steam ships of the last two centuries. We see few of them on the Mersey today, not only because they carry more cargo but also because most of them use the docks at the mouth of the river.

A few ships still pass the city waterfront to berth

at Birkenhead or head up-river to Bromborough, Garston and the Manchester Ship Canal. Even the ownership of the docks has changed hands. The former railway docks at Garston passed to Associated British Ports in 1982, and now import aggregates, cereals, fertilisers, steel and timber on coastal trade routes with Europe, and have a bagging plant for aggregates and fertilisers.

The Mersey Docks & Harbour Company took over the ports at Heysham, Sheerness and Chatham and the container terminal at Dublin between 1993 and 2001. In 2005 the company was, in turn, taken over by Peel Holdings, bringing the Manchester Ship Canal and Clyde wharves at Shieldhall, Greenock and Hunterston into the family tree. So we have lost the local ownership of the Mersey docks dating back 1857, when the former Mersey Docks & Harbour Board was established, and, further back, to 1715, when Liverpool Corporation opened the first dock.

Cargo-passenger liners no longer serve Manchester docks, but tankers and freighters still use the ship canal, mainly to serve Cheshire's petro-chemical industries and the Staffordshire potteries from wharves at Ellesmere Port, Stanlow, Runcorn, Partington, Eccles and Trafford Park. Cargoes on the ship canal dropped from the peak 18½ million tons in 1955 to 6¼ million tons by 2003, partly because of oil piped from Tranmere oil terminal, but trade is rising again. With increased imports of coal for Fiddler's Ferry power station and coastwise shipments of petroleum products, the canal shipped 7¼ million tons of cargo in 2005, slightly more than in 1947. Most of the other tonnage is also made up of bulk cargoes of chemicals, minerals, oil and scrap metal. Mersey ferries continue their excursions up the ship canal, as they have done since it opened in 1894.

It is encouraging to see the partial recovery of the Mersey ports, the clean air zones, the restored buildings, the return of ocean liners on cruises and the return of marine life to the Mersey, including cod, dolphins, porpoises, salmon, sea trout and razor fish. We even have seals in the estuary, and tourists in Birkenhead and Liverpool. But what is it all for? These advancements are wasted if our urban environment is less interesting, less congenial and less civilised.

Developers keep coming up with spectacular, high-density building schemes at the expense of our environment. Their schemes show no respect for the character of the place and the developers do not have to live there. Sacred focal points of Merseyside life, such as Birkenhead Woodside, New Brighton promenade and Liverpool Pier Head, are particularly vulnerable to insensitive redevelopment that can ruin the character of these important locations.

The Woodside master plan, referred to in Volume 1, emerged in July 2006, and in September came a massive scheme to recreate Manhattan in dockland on both sides of the Mersey with 50-storey skyscrapers that would be the biggest transformation of Merseyside in its history and the largest development project in Britain. I notice that redevelopment now always comes under the euphemistic guise of 'regeneration' to sell the idea to the local authority, but the developers are only interested in making maximum profit out of every square foot and the local councils back them to generate more Council Tax.

Can we assume that these schemes for homes, offices, shops and leisure will regenerate the economy? Merseyside of 1850 to 1950 was custom-built. The new schemes are speculative development. Who will occupy these new blocks? Has experience taught us nothing? We have demolished the high-rise flats in Birkenhead and Everton. We have empty offices to let in Liverpool's central business district and empty new offices in Birkenhead's Woodside and dockland regeneration area. The Manhattan plan would close part of Birkenhead docks to shipping and create a marina for 'tourist boats'.

The only way to attract tourists to Merseyside is to offer something different, like Vienna, Turin or Lisbon. Do we want Merseyside to look like Singapore, Shanghai, Sydney and all the other uniform clusters of skyscrapers around the world? Do we want to live in the permanent shadow of stark, glass towers? Do we want to live and work 50 storeys high? Can we risk defacing Merseyside irrevocably with huge white elephants? Should residents have to face mounting legal bills to protect their environment from the succession of heady schemes from already wealthy developers? Should local councils allow speculative developers to dictate the future shape of our towns or should councils initiate and direct sensitive redevelopment? Does anyone really care about the place any more?

Six years ago I met an old colleague from Chester who told me he had moved home to New Brighton and found it a very pleasant place to live. I envied him as I was living at Saltney at the time, and said, 'Yes, but it was far more interesting when it had a pier and a ferry.' He shrugged his shoulders and said, 'I know nothing about that.' That was what prompted me to produce this book: to show new residents – and visitors – what a great place it was not so long ago.

So now let us eclipse our present-day image of Merseyside with a portrayal of the same place but the very different scene little more than 50 years ago. Like Harry Lime's Vienna, it had been 'bombed about a bit' but it had not lost its spirit. The two world wars and the industrial unrest and recession between the wars were over, and the mid-20th century was a period of recovery and almost full employment. The dockside and shipyard cranes along the Mersey bank were in full swing, the ferry steamers and landing stages were crowded, and day-trippers and holidaymakers flocked to the sands and fairground at New Brighton. This was Merseyside in its element. But the post-war heyday was brief and there followed a long, slow run-down in the context of the decline of industrial Britain in the second half of the century. This is a portrait of Merseyside during that brief heyday.

This work is essentially a view of Merseyside from the Cheshire bank as a change from the usual view from Liverpool. This enables us to get a better perspective view of Liverpool from without rather than from within. I prefer to work up the readers' interest in the city by references and glimpses from the other side of the river and to feature Liverpool as a dramatic finale to the work.

In Volume 1 we approached Merseyside by train from Paddington to Woodside, surveyed the townscape from Port Sunlight to the docks that lie between Birkenhead and Wallasey, and crossed and recrossed the Mersey by the Birkenhead and Wallasey Ferries from Woodside to Liverpool, Seacombe and New Brighton.

Seacombe Ferry is our transit to both Wallasey and Liverpool in this volume. After the grand tour of Wallasey we return by ferry to Liverpool Pier Head, and our 'trambulation' around Liverpool brings us back to Pier Head. But Liverpool is not quite the finale. Even Liverpolitans tired of life in the city and looked longingly at the wooded ranges of hills west 'over the water'. Finally we return to the Cheshire bank to head over the hills behind Birkenhead for a short, final chapter on the rural hinterland of the Wirral peninsula between the estuaries of the Mersey and the Dee.

Most of my photographs in this book were taken on a fortnight's holiday at Wallasey between 21 August and 4 September 1954, but the earliest pictures were taken when I lived there in 1949-52, and several more were taken on annual pilgrimages to Merseyside from 1957 to 1961, when it featured on every annual holiday itinerary.

Finally, I want to tell you of an experience on a pilgrimage to Merseyside in 1959 that nicely illustrates the character of Merseysiders as they were in those happy days. This account is taken from a diary of a 16-day hitch-hiking and youth-hostelling holiday around midland and northern England and Scotland with my girlfriend, Ruth, whom I married three years later. The date was 16 May 1959, and we had just hitch-hiked from Herne Bay on the first day via the A41 from London, visiting Warwick and Chester on the way. It was Whit weekend and Chester youth hostel, then at Hoole Bank, was full.

We walked back along the lane in the lowering dusk to the Chester by-pass to hitch-hike the last stretch of the A41 to Birkenhead and go on to New Brighton to find bed and breakfast. The road was unlit and we must have been indiscernible to the drivers behind the car headlights that flashed past. I resorted to waving my handkerchief, and soon a luxurious car stopped for us. The driver and his wife were from Liverpool and the man talked to us in that clattering, guttural, rushing, slurring, sing-song Lancastrian-Dublin accent of Merseysiders. Among other things he said, 'Liverpool is a horrible place – but I love it! I've been all round the country but I still think this district is the best place to live.'

They were on their way home to Liverpool but insisted on taking us to our destination first. We glided along the broad Chester-Birkenhead road and it was not long before we were in the blue-green lamp-lit suburbs of Birkenhead and among the blue and cream Birkenhead buses. We had come to the end of the A41 route, which had led us 198 miles across England.

We crossed the glittering docks to Wallasey and our driver dropped us outside a house in Rullerton Road, where I had stayed an odd night at late notice two years before and the lady of the house had invited me to stay there again any time. The car drove away, back to Birkenhead and the tunnel. The house was in darkness. I knocked at the door; there came no answer. We walked around the corner to the Boot Inn, but they did not provide bed and breakfast.

It was nearly 11 pm on Whit Saturday, not a good time to find accommodation. We walked to the centre of Liscard, from which yellow Corporation buses on six routes diverged up two roads to New Brighton, and we soon found ourselves running to and from one road and the other after different buses and missing them all. Two big, jolly men stopped us to help. They took us to a bus stop and told us of two boarding houses in New Brighton and the names of the landladies, to whom we were to say Mac had recommended us. They chatted with us while we waited for the bus and the very last lap of our journey that day was made on the beige leather seats in its mahogany-trimmed, dimly lit interior behind a loud, guttural, roaring engine.

Through Upper Brighton we descended the steep hill into New Brighton and presented ourselves at the first house Mac recommended.

That was full. We tried the second. That had been divided into apartments but one of the tenants, a tall, fair-haired, softly spoken young man, referred us to another house in the street and accompanied us to it. A merry-looking landlady opened the door, the house looked cosy inside but she was sorry – her house was full as well, and she referred us to another house. In this way we were referred from house to house with the young man kindly accompanying and introducing us and negotiating for us. We were seventh time lucky, and the young man left us feeling weary and dirty at 11.30pm with the door open to a clean and pleasant house, a hospitable landlady and the last two vacant beds in the house. After a thorough and refreshing wash we sank in our soft, comfortable beds and deep sleep.

When I awoke next morning and looked out of my bedroom window I could see down the street to Perch Rock lighthouse standing in the placid, blue-grey waters of the Irish Sea and over the rooftops to the grey outline of Bootle docks on the other side of the river. I sniffed the air; it had that nostalgic, characteristic Wallasey tang of unimaginable salty freshness and sweetness, the strength of which I have never savoured elsewhere. The sky was bright and pale; early morning sunlight fell on the empty Sunday morning streets. After a good breakfast we set off on our tour of the three towns of the Mersey estuary – Wallasey and Birkenhead on the Cheshire bank and Liverpool on the Lancashire side – all of which I found as Emetty, dark, barbaric and fresh as ever. Welcome to Merseyside in the 1950s.

WALLASEY

As the New Brighton ferry steamed down-river from Liverpool, Wallasey lay along the left bank from Birkenhead docks to the sea. The town stands high above the river on its sandstone plateau, rising to 180 feet above the Mersey and the Irish Sea above New Brighton, then dropping to Rock Point, the north-east corner of the Wirral peninsula. The Wallasey bank was studded with landmarks: the clock tower at Seacombe Ferry, the Town Hall with its lantern tower, the clock steeple of the Mariners' Homes at Egremont, the dark-red bulk of New Brighton Tower Building with its four conical spires, and New Brighton Pier stretched out across the river mouth.

The red rock river wall and riverside promenade run all the 2¼ miles from Seacombe Ferry to New Brighton Pier. The promenade is backed by villas on banked gardens, and streets of houses rise steeply inland. The disused ferry tollhouse still stood on the abutment in the river wall where the pier of the extinct Egremont Ferry once strode into the river. Sandy beaches and flat slabs of seaweedy bedrock stretch from Egremont to New Brighton and, as we go north, the bosky riverbank streets rise steeper and higher to a plateau of rooftops and church towers among trees.

The green copper dome of the majestic Roman Catholic church above New Brighton crowns the highest point of the plateau and is an impressive landmark from incoming ships sailing up the Crosby Channel into Liverpool. The sea washes around the red sandstone fort and the white lighthouse on Perch Rock, guarding the river mouth. From the heights of New Brighton we look out across the expanse of Liverpool Bay from the sand dunes of the Lancashire coast to the mountain backdrop of north Wales.

The satanic scene of cranes and smoke-stacks of Liverpool's northern dockland on the opposite bank of the river was in stark contrast to the pleasant, middle-class, residential and seaside town on the Cheshire bank. The view from the electric train clattering over the viaduct of the Southport line between Liverpool Exchange and Bootle or rumbling along the Overhead between Pier Head and Seaforth gave alluring views between the giant warehouses and transit sheds of a land so different on the other side of the river as to be almost a mirage of another world.

The riverside townships of Seacombe, Egremont, Upper Brighton and New Brighton, together with the neighbouring inland townships of Somerville, Poulton, Liscard and Wallasey itself, are all districts of Wallasey. They are all on the plateau, which was once an island, called Wallasey. The townships retain their individual identity but also acquiesce in their collective, geographical name.

In my text it is usually obvious whether I am referring to the township of Wallasey or to the wider built-up area of the same name. When I write the name Wallasey I usually mean the township, but when I refer to the Wallasey side of the docks or the Wallasey riverbank, this is a geographical reference, as Wallasey dockland was entirely in the townships of Poulton and Seacombe, and the riverbank was in Seacombe, Egremont, Upper Brighton and New Brighton. Where the reference could be ambiguous I tend to refer to geographical Wallasey as 'the island'.

ISLAND, TOWNSHIP AND COUNTY BOROUGH

Wallasey is on a peninsula within a peninsula. It was an island in the Mersey estuary when the English King Æthelfrith of Northumbria split the Celtic alliance between Cambria and Cumbria at the battle of Chester, circa 613 AD, and the Celts of Wirral took refuge on what the English called 'Wealas-ey', the Welshmen's island. (The names Wales and Welsh are derived from 'wealas', which was not a proper name but simply the old English word for strangers or foreigners.) Wallasey is a possessive name – Wallas'-ey – so it was spelt phonetically Wallazee or Wallazey on old maps and records, as the old Cheshire people pronounced it (like the rock islands Bardsey, Ramsey and Guernsey, and the marsh island Bermondsey). It was the settlers from Liverpool in the 19th century who called it Walla-sea.

The insular plateau of red and yellow sandstone became attached to the mainland by alluvial salt marshes on the west, where Leasowe and Moreton are now. This 'mossland' was not drained till the construction of Birkenhead docks in the mid-19th century, and was still subject to flooding at high water into the early 20th century. Where the Mersey once flowed to the sea, there was now a tidal creek, Wallasey Pool, on the south. Walea, Walsey, Walayesegh or Wallazey, as it was variously written, was a place of farmland, heath, cliffs and dunes, with cottages gathered together in four farming and fishing villages: 'Wallasey for wreckers, Poulton for trees, Liscard for honest men and Seacombe for thieves,' as the old saying went. There was a cluster of fishermen's shacks on Rock Point, now New Brighton.

These four villages were all in the ancient parish of Wallasey. The parish church was founded circa 446 by Bishop (later Saint) Germanus of Gaul, a missionary to the Britons in 440-450, shortly before the Anglo-Saxon invasions brought English dominion over the land. Wallasey church is one of only eight churches in Britain dedicated to St Hilary, six of them in Wales and Cornwall. Thus a Celtic church was established in Wallasey before it became a refuge from the English. Liscard is a Celtic place name and Poulton and Seacombe contain Celtic place name elements. St Hilary is an appropriate dedication as he is usually depicted standing on an island.

Norse colonists from Ireland and the Isle of Man settled the eastern littoral of the Irish Sea from the Solway to Anglesey between 890 and 920, landing in Wirral in 904. A hardy, seafaring race of fishermen and fell-farmers, they were content to settle the coastal fringes and upland heath and not stray too far from the sea, as can be seen from the place names ending with -by. Wallasey Pool, Hoylake and the firth of Dee harboured their longships. Thingwall ('assembly field') was the site of the parliament and court for the coastal settlements from the Ribble to the Dee (like Tynwald in Man and Thingvellir in Iceland). Bromborough, on the Mersey ('boundary river'), between English Mercia and the then Scandinavian kingdom of York, is a contender for

the site of the Battle of Brunanburgh in 937, when the English of Mercia and Wessex defeated a combined force of Norse, Irish and Scots for the dominion of northern England. (Bromborough and Mersey are both English names.)

The Norsemen had a way of telling the difference between Wallasey and Wallasey; they called the island Walley and the village Kirkby-in-Walley, 'the church village in the Welshmen's island'. The village was still marked Kirkby-in-Walley on maps right down to 1611, but by 1665 it had reverted to the same name as the island and was written 'Wallazey'.

Under the Normans, Wallasey was listed in the Domesday Book, the national survey of economic resources for taxation by King William I in 1086, when Birkenhead and Liverpool were so insignificant as not to be mentioned.

The three-quarter-mile ferry passage from Seacombe to Liverpool was first recorded in 1330. In the 16th and 17th centuries Poulton, on Wallasey Pool, rivalled the port of Liverpool for shipping. In the 18th and early 19th centuries Wallasey was notorious for wreckers and smugglers. Wreckers were said to have lured ships on to the sandbanks with bonfires, robbed the survivors and plundered the cargoes. Fishermen smuggled rum, salt, sugar and tobacco ashore till the hefty import duties on those commodities were lifted.

The history of Wallasey is to be found in the records of its ancient church and the stories of its four thatched, stone inns that existed in the 16th century – the Seacombe Boat House, the Pool Inn at Poulton, the Boot Inn at Liscard and the Cheshire Cheese in Wallasey – not forgetting Mother Redcap's (1595), which became an inn about 1780. The stories of Mother Redcap's and the Boot Inn are told in the text under the photographs. Some old Wallasey inns were demolished for road widening in the 1920s and '30s and replaced by new inns built behind them; the Wellington and Boot at Liscard and the Cheshire Cheese and Black Horse at Wallasey come to mind. The old Cheshire Cheese, which narrowed the village street to 6 feet, survived till the 1880s, when it was demolished for road widening and the present Cheshire Cheese Inn was built. The old Black Horse of 1722 survived till

1931. The name of this hotel is thought to commemorate one of Lord Molyneux's horses in the races that were Wallasey's greatest claim to fame in history.

One of England's earliest racecourses, existing in the 17th and 18th centuries, was a 5-mile course along the leasowes, an old English name for the meadows between the marshes and the coastal dunes west of Wallasey. The start and finish was at the north end of the village and the horses turned back at the octagonal tower of Leasowe Castle, built in 1593 for the Stanleys, Earls of Derby, who laid out the course. The first recorded race was run in 1637 and the races were patronised by the nobility and gentry, including the Dukes of Devonshire and Bridgewater. The Duke of Monmouth rode his own horse to victory in 1682, and racing stables in the village were owned by the Stanleys, Molyneux and Grosvenors. The first sweepstakes in England were run by a group of Cheshire gentry at Wallasey in 1723. The racecourse closed about 1760-85 as racing moved to Melling, then Aintree. Wallasey Stakes went to Newmarket, then Epsom, where they continue as the Derby Stakes.

At the first census in 1801 the population of the four villages in the parish of Wallasey was only 663, but that was six times more than Birkenhead. These villages could only be approached by land along Green Lane on the leasowes. The advent of steam ferries led to new villa settlements at Egremont from 1830 and at New Brighton from 1834 for Liverpool merchants, ship-owners and industrialists coming to live in healthier rural retreats on the Cheshire bank. Wallasey developed much more slowly than Birkenhead after the arrival of steam ferries and provided sanctuary for the villa residents from urbanisation for much longer because of its insular situation.

The second road access was a wooden toll-bridge erected over Wallasey Pool at Poulton in 1843 at the end of a causeway laid across the moss from Bidston. Samuel Lewis's 1848 survey records that 92 per cent of Wallasey was still under cultivation. The 1851 census gave the population of the island as 8,348, now only one-third that of burgeoning Birkenhead. An 1851 map of Wallasey shows that it was still entirely rural in the mid-19th century, with only isolated terraces at Seacombe and Egremont. William Herdman's paintings show that Seacombe was still a picturesque village in the 1860s.

Picturesque as it was, rural Seacombe was found by a Government inspector there in 1851 to have a mortality rate worse than the industrial slums of Liverpool because of poor housing conditions, contaminated well water and inadequate sewage disposal. The damming of Wallasey Pool for docks had impounded sewage from Seacombe that had previously been washed away by the tides. The inspector found that sanitation and mortality in the rest of Wallasey was just as bad. There was no public water supply, no street lighting and the streets were filthy. The Wallasey Improvement Commissioners, elected in 1845, had been torpid; they were not men of vision like the Improvement Commissioners of Birkenhead. As a result of the inspector's report, the Commissioners were sacked and a Local Board of Health was elected in 1853. From 1863 treated water was supplied from Gorsehill reservoir, New Brighton, and Mill Lane water tower, Liscard.

Construction of docks in Wallasey Pool had begun at Woodside in 1844. The opening of the dock crossings in the 1860s ended Wallasey's isolation and led to the industrialisation of the southern fringe of Seacombe and Poulton. Dockland development combined with the public ownership of the ferries from 1861, which gave regular, reliable services, cheap tolls, floating landing stages and saloon steamers – these were the catalysts for the urban growth of Wallasey and its complete transformation from a rural retreat to a county borough within 50 years. The tardy development of this rural corner of Merseyside is reflected in the relatively late arrival of the railway at Wallasey and New Brighton in 1888 and at Poulton and Seacombe in 1895 – later than in rural north Norfolk. The Seacombe branch became a western outpost of the London & North Eastern Railway.

The causeway (now Tower Road) along the dam across Wallasey Pool to Seacombe opened in 1860, and the Four Bridges were installed along it in 1866-67. Duke Street Bridge opened in 1861, but Gorsey Lane remained unpaved till Woodstock Road opened in 1924 as the last link in the main road into Wallasey. Thus the first horse-buses from Birkenhead, in 1903, plied over the Four Bridges between Charing Cross and Seacombe, and the first joint Corporation motorbus service, in 1921, was routed via Duke Street Bridge and Dock Road to Seacombe. Later the same year a Charing Cross-Liscard bus service had to go via Duke Street Bridge, Poulton and Mill Lane because of the missing link for the direct route. The third dock crossing, the old toll-bridge at Poulton, was not replaced by a toll-free swing-bridge till 1926, prior to the final dock extension to Bidston Dock in 1933 in what remained of the natural creek.

The peak of development came in the late-Victorian and Edwardian period, which saw the population rocket to 78,504 by 1911. Most of the rustic, thatched stone cottages of Seacombe, Poulton, Liscard and Wallasey disappeared as urbanisation spread from Seacombe Ferry and dockland. The new township of Somerville appeared between Seacombe and Poulton, named after Somerville House on the site of Hallville Road, and Upper Brighton grew up on the summit of the new road approaches to New Brighton by way of Rake Lane and Seabank Road, making a total of eight townships or districts in the built-up area on the plateau.

Wallasey itself retained its village character into Edwardian times, with a very narrow main street of irregular stone cottages and farm buildings, gardens and hedges. While Seacombe, Liscard and New Brighton had electric tramways in 1902, Wallasey was still served by horse-buses till 1911, when the electric cars began to ply along new tramroads (Marlowe Road and Claremount Road) between fields that still divided Wallasey from Liscard and Poulton, and the line by-passed the narrow village street on widened back lanes (Broadway, St George's Road and Sandy Lane).

I saw the last stretch of the old Wallasey village street being demolished in 1950; it was a gloomy, narrow defile of plain, grey stone, rural slum cottages between the top of Leasowe Road and the bottom of Sandy Lane. Several 17th- and 18th-century sandstone buildings of rural Wallasey remain, notably the old rectory on Church Hill, the small cottage in Breck Road, which was the second Wallasey Grammar School from 1799 to 1864, Bird's House in Limekiln Lane, Poulton, a stone terrace in Manor Road, Liscard, and cottages in Magazine Brow, Upper Brighton.

Wallasey street names retain something of the rural character of the area before urbanisation. Wallasey Village is the name of the main street of Wallasey. The street nameplates define the limits of the former one-street village, just as Liscard Village is the former village street of Liscard. Lanes and footpaths shown on the 1851 map are remembered today in Gorsey Lane, Green Lane (Wallasey), Greenwood Lane (late Green Lane, Liscard), Limekiln Lane, Love Lane, Magazine Lane, Manor Lane, Martin's Lane, Mill Lane, Rake Lane, Rice Lane, Sandy Lane, Sherlock Lane, Wheatland Lane and Withens Lane.

The Local Board of Health took over the ferries in 1861 and the growth of the town in late-Victorian and Edwardian times is reflected in it becoming, in rapid succession, an Urban District in 1894, a Municipal Borough in 1910 and an all-purpose County Borough in 1913. The County Borough of Wallasey existed for 61 years till local government re-organisation in 1974, and Wallasey Town Hall is still the seat of local government of an equally autonomous north Wirral district with equivalent county borough status.

Thus, in the period I am writing of, there were three entities with the name of Wallasey: 1) the compact built-up area of the eight townships (pop 90,809) on the plateau that was once an island; 2) the former village, now a township (pop 12,541), on the west side of the plateau; and 3) the County Borough (pop 101,331) extending to Leasowe, Moreton and Saughall Massie on the low-lying, alluvial land to the west. (The populations are taken from Bartholomew's Gazetteer after the 1951 census.)

Wallasey is still bounded by water on three sides, on the south by the docks, on the east by the Mersey and on the north by the Irish Sea. In the mid-20th century Bidston Moss on the west was a no-man's-land of drained marshes, golf links, railway junctions, sidings and steelworks. Wallasey's only physical link with the outside world, apart from the dock bridges, was the causeway along Leasowe Road, paralleling the old Green Lane. Wallasey is, as one local author called it in the title of his book, almost an island. Unlike Birkenhead, it is on the road to nowhere but

Wallasey. The only motor traffic is local. In the mid-20th century motor coaches filed through the town to New Brighton, otherwise the wide roads of Wallasey were pleasantly empty and quiet. But there was nearly always a bus in sight.

This was a time when Wallasey Corporation had a fleet of 90 double-deckers, and these primrose and cream buses were a regular sight as they plied the 20 Corporation bus routes that served this residential town and seaside resort on the Cheshire coast. Mum said that a Wallasey bus was 'like a ray of sunshine coming along the road'. Of the 20 bus routes, 11 converged on Seacombe Ferry from New Brighton, Wallasey, Moreton and Birkenhead. Four of these routes started and finished at the same terminals in New Brighton and Seacombe, serving different parts of the town on the way.

SEACOMBE

It was ferry time in Wallasey. It was always ferry time in Wallasey in those days because the buses were timed to meet the ferries at Seacombe every 15 minutes through the day, and every 10 minutes at peak periods. All day long the big wheels were rolling down to Seacombe as the tall buses descended from the salubrious heights of New Brighton and Wallasey into the mean, drab streets of Seacombe. The buses converged on the steamboat station just in time for passengers to buy their tickets and walk straight on board the ferry to Liverpool, which ran at the same intervals as the buses.

The pulse of Wallasey was synchronised with ferry sailings from Seacombe, as about half the working population was employed in Liverpool. Ferry time was shown on a clock dial on the back platform of each bus, and the conductor set the hands to the time of the ferry the bus connected with. The Corporation buses and ferries could be relied upon to run on time and to connect at Seacombe in a way that they were not scheduled to connect at Woodside or Liverpool. The combined service was so reliable and efficient that some Liverpool waterfront businessmen came home to Wallasey for midday dinner.

The Corporation buses were run like the Royal Navy. The journey was punctuated by the conductor alighting from his back platform to register the departure time from time stages with a 'clunk-zhing' in the roadside time clocks that were sited at strategic bus stops, and made sure that the buses did not run before time. Sometimes this meant a short wait to register the right departure time. Otherwise it was a clear run with the conductor collecting the fares from the seated and standing passengers, no traffic congestion and only five sets of road signals in the whole borough.

The Seacombe Ferry bus ritual was another of the routine daily dramas on Merseyside, and the setting was one of the architectural highlights of Wallasey. The classical, Portland-stone colonnades of the ferry buildings of 1930-33 line two sides of Victoria Place, dominated by the 90-foot red-brick, Art Deco clock tower rising above the grand, central, Romanesque stone arch of the tollhouse. It appeared suddenly as we rounded the curves from humble Demesne Street, Church Street and Birkenhead Road and rumbled over the broad plain of granite setts at the ferry approach. We glimpsed the black, smoking stacks of north Liverpool dockland across the river from Seacombe Promenade as the bus swung round the corner of the square and rolled up to the colonnade of the tollhouse to drop the passengers outside the great central arch. As they alighted we heard the pennies clattering into the uncollected fares box on the conductor's platform after a peak-time journey with a full, standing load. The bus then pulled round the next corner of the square and reversed up to the loading colonnade, the driver slamming on the brake as the conductor blasted on his whistle at the kerb.

Depending on the time of day, anything from eight to 17 buses arrived in close succession within 4 minutes, sometimes forming up to three abreast to unload at the tollhouse, then backing up to the loading colonnade one after the other to line up in herringbone order. Studs in the granite setts marked out the loading bays and the route numbers for 17 buses, including peak-time short-workings, on ten routes here in Victoria Place. The 11th route was a joint Birkenhead service across the dock bridges and was not timed to meet the ferry; that loaded around the corner of the colonnade in Birkenhead Road.

The crowds from the ferry were waiting under the colonnade to board the buses as soon as they backed up. The last bus to arrive was loaded within 2 minutes. Then the clanky Westminster chimes of Seacombe Ferry clock sounded the hour or the quarter-hour. The duty inspector blew his whistle, the drivers' cab doors slammed in quick succession and the buses left in an orderly convoy, lumbering off up the slope of Church Street like elephants nose-to-tail, to disperse to various parts of the borough, leaving Victoria Place empty. Shortly after they had gone, more buses came bounding in over the granite setts to meet the next ferry, and we would witness the same procedure 15 minutes later. At peak times this ritual took place every 10 minutes, then the clock chimes preceded the inspector's whistle only on the hour and half-hour.

THE MERSEY BANK

The riverside promenade begins at Seacombe Ferry and extends 2¼ miles to New Brighton Pier. This is a promenade in the true sense of the word, which means walk, both noun and verb, as this promenade was made for walking; although paved and lit like an ordinary road, it was strictly for pedestrians. It was 45 feet wide with a sealed carriageway and flagstone footpaths with kerbs, ordinary street lamps and dark green railings atop the river wall. All but the last 100 yards to New Brighton Pier was reserved for pedestrians, lovers, perambulators and roller-skaters, being closed to all vehicles except for Corporation service vehicles. I was not even allowed to ride my bicycle on the promenade. Although there were no vehicles, the orderly and well-dressed pedestrians of the period still kept to the footpaths. (It is still a pedestrian reservation today, flush-paved right across with the addition of a marked cycle path.)

The rock-faced, red sandstone river wall and the promenade were built between 1891 and 1901 in a commendable, municipal enterprise to buy all the land along the river bank to stop erosion of the clay cliffs and give public access to the shore. The promenade was extended from New Brighton Pier around the corner of Rock Point and along the seafront to Wallasey Beach between 1906 and 1939. Wallasey's riverside promenade was – and still is – the most pleasant walk on Merseyside. This is not only a traffic-free promenade but a residential promenade. There are no bright lights,

no petrol fumes, no amusement arcades, no smell of chips – just us, the trees, houses and gardens, the river, the fresh salty air and the ships.

The Mersey bank promenade was justly celebrated in the New Brighton, Wallasey guide book of the time as the 'grandstand of world shipping'. The river widens from half a mile at Seacombe to a mile at its mouth at New Brighton, and Liverpool's northern docks line the opposite bank of the river, so from the promenade we had a wide view of the constant movement of incoming and outgoing liners and freighters to and from all the Mersey docks and the Manchester Ship Canal, together with the tugs, ferries, dredgers and fishing-boats moving up and down the river.

On our left the banked villa gardens and steep side streets (with bollards across the bottom) are ranged all the way from Seacombe to New Brighton. The riverside promenade is Wallasey's favourite amenity, and many of Wallasey's other amenities were ranged along it (some of these have since disappeared). Seacombe steamboat station itself was impressive in its architecture and spaciousness. North of the ferry we passed, ranged along the cliff top, North Seacombe Recreation Ground, the Edwardian red-brick Guinea Gap Baths, and the majestic grey-stone Wallasey Town Hall facing the river atop its great flight of steps.

The prospect along the river bank between Seacombe and New Brighton was divided into two slight bays by Egremont Ferry Hotel, and the shuttered ferry tollhouse jutted out on a small bluff and abutment in the river wall, dreaming of the high days of the pier and ferry that had all come to an end with the war. North of Egremont Ferry the fine, sandy shore was popular in summer with Wallasey residents, and Egremont Promenade was backed by trees, with the 135-foot-tall clock steeple of the Home For Aged Mariners peering over the treetops of their private park. The site of the Mariners' Homes was well chosen to give retired merchant officers a view of the maritime scene that had been their life. Next we came to Mother Redcap's Café (1595 to 1974), formerly an inn, the most historic house in Wallasey, with its ghosts of ancient mariners, smugglers and privateers, but the old house was now heavily disguised as a late-Victorian picturesque villa.

The line of trees stretched all the way from

Egremont to New Brighton. Magazines Promenade, Upper Brighton, is the most pleasant part of the entire walk. The riverside villas become more diverse in architecture as we move into the late-Victorian and Edwardian period and they are set back from the promenade behind a belt of public gardens, in which Wallasey's modest cenotaph of 1920 is sited at the corner of Magazine Lane with its statuesque heroes looking out across the river. The lovely Vale Park, with its tall trees, hillocks and classical domed bandstand, slopes down to the promenade between Magazine Lane and Vaughan Road.

A short way up the steep slope of granite setts at the foot of Magazine Lane we find two strange buildings set among the ordinary houses: the small, conical-roofed watchman's roundhouse of the former gunpowder magazines used by sailing ships in the Mersey from circa 1765 to 1851, and the castellated gateway of the former Liscard Battery (1858 to 1912). Inter-war semi-detached houses now sit rather incongruously inside the stone walls of the fort. The roundhouse and the fort gate face each other across the entrance of Magazine Brow, which, in its winding undulations, features several old stone cottages and, to this day, retains the character of a village street.

The whole of Upper Brighton, from Magazines Promenade to Earlston Road, is the least altered part of Wallasey. The district is mainly Edwardian, centred around two shopping streets along the north end of Seabank Road and the top of Rowson Street. The promenade is distinctive in being the only section of the riverside walk with houses set back behind a belt of public gardens, which begin and end at the old ward boundaries between Egremont Promenade and Tower Promenade, New Brighton.

NEW BRIGHTON

As Magazines Promenade gives on to Tower Promenade we enter New Brighton alongside the Tower Amusement Park. The line of trees and gardens continued as the setting for the quaint, steamy Fairy Glen Railway, an 18-inch narrow-gauge line of unusual quality for a seaside fairground ride with its tunnel and waterwheel, live steam engines and enclosed bogie coaches with upholstered seats and electric lights. The railway was a feature of New Brighton from 1948 to 1965 and I feel that these dates reflect the post-war rise and demise of New Brighton as a seaside resort.

From the treetops north of the Fairy Glen Railway we heard the rumble and screams of the Scenic Railway, a roller-coaster ride on a multi-storey, figure-of-eight, wooden trestle. Both railways were part of the permanent fairground, with a small zoo, on the steep slopes below the Tower Building. An athletics stadium behind the Tower Building was the home of New Brighton Football & Athletic Club from 1946 to 1976. The club, formerly in Sandheys Park, Upper Brighton, played in the Third Division North of the Football League from 1923 to 1951. The Tower Building (1900 to 1969) was a massive, dark-red-brick pile, topped with pyramids and cupolas, housing a ballroom and theatre that were among the largest in Britain. The building dominated New Brighton long after the Tower had disappeared from the Mersey scene.

The Tower Building was the base of New Brighton Tower, a lattice steel tower like Blackpool's. Designed by the same architects and built in 1897-1900, it was not only taller than Blackpool Tower but octagonal in section and more graceful. It stood 562 feet tall on a slope 59 feet above the sea, its topmost pinnacle reaching 621 feet above sea level, 121 feet higher than Blackpool's. In its time New Brighton Tower was the highest structure in Britain and, of course, Merseyside's largest landmark, a conspicuous goalpost for everyone bound for New Brighton in Edwardian times. Its glory was short-lived, being closed in 1914 for the First World War, when neglect made it unsafe, and dismantled in 1919-21.

The traffic-free promenade ends in a line of bollards alongside the Tower Grounds, and the next 1¼ miles of promenades from here to Wallasey Beach are used by motor traffic. Next to the Tower Grounds was the Tivoli Theatre (1914 to 1955), with its central dome and two tall, flat-topped pyramids on its twin corner towers. The theatre, with its glazed iron colonnade over the six shops flanking the entrance, spanned the block between Egerton Street and Tollemache Street. Once the most successful vaudeville theatre on Merseyside and a cinema in 1923-30, the Tivoli had reverted to a live theatre and was staging twice nightly variety shows in summer and repertory in the winter in the post-war period. It was the only Merseyside theatre or cinema on the waterfront.

From the Tower, the fairground and the Tower Promenade we looked out over a sandy beach, sometimes crowded, with well-dressed people not daring to expose themselves to the rarefied northern sunlight. There were mobile stalls selling shellfish and mineral waters, donkey rides and a small, tidal, boating and paddling pool with paddle-boats to hire. Offshore, a short distance up-river of the pier, were the moorings of the New Brighton lifeboat and the last flotilla of the Liverpool fishing fleet, a dozen or more Lancashire 'nobbies', with 'LL' (Liverpool) and their port registration numbers in white on their tall, brown sails.

We came at last to New Brighton Pier, the landmark of our riverside walk from Seacombe, to find that what we have until now referred to as the pier was actually two piers alongside – two parallel, iron piers with an almost parallel history: the Ferry Pier (built 1867, closed 1971, demolished 1973), and the higher and wider Promenade Pier (built 1867, closed 1972, demolished 1978).

At New Brighton Piers the view changed completely. Appropriately, from the Ferry Pier we had an up-river prospect of Liverpool, while from the Promenade Pier we gazed out on the open sea. Beyond here the promenade extension of 1906-08, Marine Promenade, curved around Rock Point on the Cheshire corner of the Mersey and the Irish Sea and our prospect from the promenade changed from north Liverpool docks to the horizon of the sea in Liverpool Bay, framed between the Lancashire coastal dunes and the mountains of north Wales.

The word 'STEAMERS' was displayed in lights across a gantry over the entrance to the Ferry Pier, and the tollhouse was halfway along. The Promenade Pier had a 130-foot-wide deck for promenading, with two ornate rotundas jettied out on the north side. It was originally detached from the promenade and accessible only by a ramp from the Ferry Pier, but from 1900 it had its own ramped entrance direct from the promenade, rather like going aboard a ship. The Ferry Pier was always owned by the local council. The Promenade Pier

was privately owned and suffered decay. It was closed from 1923 to 1930, being bought, restored and re-opened by Wallasey Corporation.

The two pier entrances were at the foot of the main street, Victoria Road, so as you walked off the ferry you faced the wide, bell-mouth entrance of a tree-lined street of shops sloping uphill, guarded by two distinguished buildings: the cream, stuccoed, Italianate-style Royal Ferry Hotel on the corner of Tower Promenade, and the quaint, Edwardian, red-brick Avondale Café with its lantern cupola on the corner of Marine Promenade. Storey's large Bon Marché fancy goods shop occupied the ground floor of the Avondale Café building under an ornate, glazed iron colonnade extending right around the block from Marine Promenade to Virginia Road bus station. These iron colonnades, like the one we have seen at the Tivoli Theatre, were a feature of shopping streets in the other townships of Wallasey.

The lower end of the main street was all cafés, fish and chip shops, gift shops and pin-table saloons – all manna for the holidaymakers and day-trippers. Most of these places were shuttered through the winter like the hibernating fairground, and that was the way I preferred New Brighton because I was not a gregarious boy. Even with the crowds and the fairground, I liked New Brighton because of its position on the corner of the Mersey and the Irish Sea, because of its piers and ferry, its narrow-gauge steam railway, its Ghost Train, and because its fanciful Edwardian seaside architecture gave it a certain quaintness. However, I preferred New Brighton in the winter. It was quainter still when the wind rattled the shutters on the shops and fairground, the waves crashed over the promenades and the Emetty iron shelters jutted out into the wild, raging sea with white horses racing past the offshore fort and lighthouse under lowering clouds.

One of my favourite memories of New Brighton was my first early-morning cycle ride from Wallasey. From the age of 12 I had an imaginary steam bus and tram company – the Wallasey & District Steam Traction Company – with quaint old vehicles plying routes through the most characteristic streets of Wallasey and Birkenhead and out into the lanes and cart tracks of our rural hinterland. I cycled the schedules and sketched locations with the buses and trams in a quaint style, inspired by the drawings of Emett and Trog. I found beauty in the early morning, from darkness to bright sunlight, when the streets were empty and quiet and the air was fresh, so I used to take an early morning shift.

That morning I took the first service from Liscard at 4.10am, when it was still pitch dark. There were no streetlights on after midnight in those days; it was only in the early 1970s that the lights were left on all night for security. My parents might have thought I was a bit mad, but apparently they did not conceive there was any risk in 1950 for a boy going out on his own at that time and, of course, there was not. My only aid to navigation was my dim, dynamo-driven headlamp, so when I stopped I was in complete darkness and I could hardly see a hand in front of my face.

I found that I was not the only one up and about at this early hour. On my way through Liscard and Upper Brighton I nearly bumped into groups of postmen slowly cycling three-abreast without lights and, when I stopped in Victoria Road, New Brighton, and my light went out, to drink in the darkness and silence of the main street, a policeman came up to find out what I was doing out at that time of the morning. He agreed that this was the nicest time of the day and we both went on our ways. Down by the pier the darkness and silence were broken only by the chug-chug of a dimly lit bucket-ladder dredger off the Ferry Pier, either removing the silt from the ferry berth or dredging the main shipping channel. After that, I made early morning sorties on my bicycle around Wallasey and rural Wirral several times during the school holidays, returning home after 8 o'clock for breakfast.

Most of the shops for the residents of New Brighton, such as butchers, fishmongers and greengrocers, were at the upper end of the main street. New Brighton was begun in the early 1830s with a prospectus to develop a 'fashionable watering place' of detached villas on virgin heath and dunes in the north of the manor or civil parish of Liscard on the corner of the river and the sea. The plan was for detached villas to be built along streets 45 feet wide rising from both shores and intersecting at right angles. Victoria Road began as a cutting through the sand dunes to carry supplies from the original wooden ferry pier of 1834 to the villas or 'marine residences' on the hill in what are now Montpellier Crescent and Wellington Road.

Taking advantage of the contours, the early villas and terraces of New Brighton were built with uninterrupted views of the sea. What appear to be one- and two-storey villas fronting Wellington Road are two- and three-storey buildings at the back with gardens sloping steeply down the bank. The south side of Victoria Road was built in the mid-19th century with uninterrupted views of the sea for 50 years before the north side of the street was completed. The professional classes who settled on the healthy heights of New Brighton as a sanctuary from the industrial spread of Liverpool were eventually repelled by the invasion of day-trippers from Liverpool and the development of New Brighton with terraced houses for the masses just as others had been driven out of the original villa settlements of Birkenhead and Rock Ferry by the encroachment of industry.

Seaward of the pier, the spacious Marine Promenade makes a 90-degree curve around Rock Point from the river to the sea. Elegant bench seats and three ornate Edwardian iron shelters on abutments in the rock-faced, red-sandstone sea wall gave free, grandstand views of ships of the Seven Seas appearing and disappearing over the horizon and parading past, through the navigation channel in the mouth of the river. The close-up views of the passing ships with Bootle docks behind was a rather incongruous backdrop to people playing on the broad, sandy beach below the promenade and pier. The occasional transit of Army vehicles along the causeway at low water to Fort Perch Rock – still occupied by the Army till 1954 – added to the unusual attractions of New Brighton as a seaside resort.

Marine Promenade extends to Marine Park, below Wellington Road. From Seacombe Ferry to Marine Park the promenades were Wallasey's best man-made amenity. Beyond Marine Parade, until the 1930s, stretched a fine, sandy shore, backed by highly stratified sandstone cliffs with caves, the bluffs of Yellow Noses and Red Noses in yellow and red sandstone, and sand dunes that stretched from the Red Noses for a mile to Wallasey Beach, St Nicholas Church and beyond. These cliffs and sands were Wallasey's best natural amenity but they were lost and embedded in the King's Parade extension of the promenade from Marine Park to Wallasey Beach in the 1930s – only the tops of the Noses remain above ground. From the aesthetic and townscape viewpoint, this was a promenade too far.

King's Parade was retained by a huge, ugly sea wall that cut off access to the beach and blocked the view of the sea. A channel formed along the foot of the wall like a moat barring the way to the beach from the steps cut into the wall at intervals. A massive concrete parapet, instead of railings, blocked the view of the sea to promenaders and slatted wooden seats set into recesses in the parapet faced inland the full length of King's Parade – 1¼ miles of continuous seating that was hardly ever used. King's Parade was something of a 'white elephant'.

On the credit side the scheme included some real improvements. It transformed the seafront of Wallasey on a grand scale that only the 1930s could conceive and gave us the Marine Lake, the famous New Brighton Bathing Pool, the model yacht pond, the widest open spaces in Wallasey and the Derby Bathing Pool above Wallasey Beach. This municipal magnanimity was coupled with state aid to relieve the unemployment of the decade. Above all, the construction of King's Parade helped to stabilise the loose dunes and stopped the nuisance of blown sand, as we shall see later.

This scheme must be seen as part of an even more ambitious package of municipal empire-building stemming from an Act of Parliament that enabled the Corporation in 1928 to buy the Promenade Pier and to extend the County Borough west to take in Leasowe and Moreton. It was Lionel Wilkinson, Borough Engineer from 1923 to 1945 and author of the new Seacombe Ferry terminus of 1930-33, who masterminded the entire seafront scheme of 1931-39 and the rebuilding of the Promenade Pier in 1928-30. With these schemes he altered the face of Wallasey more than any other single person, but war prevented the Corporation from completing its conception of 'Britain's premier garden city by the sea'. The new promenade itself was 130 feet wide and retrospectively widened the west end of Marine Promenade from the foot of Waterloo

Road to the west end of Marine Park. The Marine Lake (1933), off Marine Promenade, impounds 10 acres of seawater at high tide between the old promenade wall, the causeway to Fort Perch Rock and the new sea wall alignment of King's Parade, embracing the site of the bathing pool. The bathing pool (1934 to 1990) was a modern, Art Deco stadium that was said to be the largest open-air swimming pool in the world, and was the scene of the Miss New Brighton bathing beauty contest from 1949 to 1989.

The model yacht pond at New Brighton was a favourite spot of mine as a boy. I spent hours there sailing my toy yacht and helping my sister sail hers. Most of the toy yachts on the pond in those days were Star Yachts, made in Birkenhead. The yacht pond is on an apron of reclaimed land for the new seafront. To me there could be no more pleasant place to be than out here in these wide open spaces in the sunshine and fresh air with the Victorian 'marine villas' atop their banked gardens on the old cliffs behind us and the view over the sea wall of Liverpool Bay and the Mersey shipping before us.

I think that Magazines Promenade, Upper Brighton, and the model yacht pond at New Brighton are still the most pleasant places on Merseyside today. If there are fewer ships in the channel, the model yacht pond is now a model ship pond, and a magnet for radio-controlled model shipbuilders recreating the great maritime tradition of Merseyside. The setting is unchanged from the 1950s, or the mid-1930s, except that the single-storey elevation of the bathing pool has gone. A little further west the stratified sandstone tops of the Yellow Noses and Red Noses, half buried by the reclamation, still peer above the wide grassland behind King's Parade.

WALLASEY TOWNSCAPE

The Wallasey plateau slopes up from the docks through Seacombe and Poulton, levelling out about 100 feet high at Liscard, then rising to 150 feet in Upper Brighton and topping 180 feet in the area between Mount Road and Atherton Street, New Brighton. There is a ridge along the west side of the plateau in Wallasey crowned by the majestic black parish church of St Hilary, with Claremount Road as the ridgeway and the former village street nestling along the foot of the west slope. The plateau is flanked by steep escarpments and the streets fall away dramatically to the Mersey on the east, to the sea on the north and to the flat fens on the west.

Most people saw Wallasey from the beige leather seats and mahogany window frames of a Corporation bus as it brushed the trees and swayed over the hills and round the bends on their way to and from work, the cinema or the beach. William Gladstone, Liverpool's famous parliamentarian, said that there was no better way to see London than from the top of a bus – and he was referring to open-top horse-buses. As the No 1 rolled along King Street and Seabank Road the views down the succession of streets to the river became higher and steeper as we gradually ascended to Upper Brighton, and there seemed to be a ship or fishing-boat on the river down every street. Then came the long, steep plunge down Rowson Street into New Brighton, with the sea ahead. Passengers on routes 14 or 15 arrived in New Brighton slightly more dramatically, down the upper part of Rowson Street or the middle section of Atherton Street. From the higher parts of New Brighton, Atherton Street and Portland Street plummet down long 1 in 12 and 1 in 8 gradients to the seafront, levelling out at intervals as they cross streets cut into the terraced hillside.

Route 17 was the grand tour of the island, taking the longest of the five routes between Seacombe and New Brighton, via Poulton and Wallasey. Along the ridgeway of Claremount Road the bus listed to port as it dipped through the junctions with Broadway and Mayfield Road, dropping steeply down the west escarpment. When we turned into Sandy Lane, the ground dropped away below us and we descended the escarpment ourselves, levelling out in time to stop at the main street, Wallasey Village. Route 2, from Seacombe via Liscard, dropped into Wallasey down St Hilary Brow, cut through the rock cliff with sheer walls towering on both sides.

As the plateau rises from south to north so does the quality of housing and the environment, from the small terraced houses with backyards and front doors opening on to the streets of Seacombe, through the bay-windowed terraced houses with small gardens front and back and the semi-

detached houses with larger gardens, until we get to the large, detached villas in their own grounds on the heights of New Brighton. Even the mean streets of Seacombe on the edge of dockland were not as grim as could be found in Birkenhead, Liverpool or the Lancashire mill towns. St Paul's Road, on the approach to the ferry, was lined with trees planted along the footpaths. The wide, quiet tree-lined streets of this town on a peninsula at the end of a peninsula remained quiet and uncluttered by cars long after the de-rationing of petrol in 1950 and the motormania of the 1960s plagued other towns.

There is an identifiable vernacular architecture about Merseyside's residential streets and shops that distinguishes this conurbation from anywhere else, and this style is most clearly defined in Wallasey. Although the old Wirral vernacular was solid stone cottages and halls rather than the timber-framed buildings that are characteristic of Cheshire, Wallasey is in the belt of late-Victorian Tudor revival architecture along the coastal lowlands from West Kirby to Southport, half-timbered with black and white, decorative (ie superficial) timber framing above red brick – Ruabon brick in Cheshire, Accrington brick in Lancashire. The particular vernacular architecture of Wallasey today is seen in the Edwardian terraces of red or yellow pressed brick with varied compositions of decorative timber framing, battlements, corner towers and turrets with conical or hexagonal spirelets like candle snuffers. These features are exemplified in Vaughan Road and surrounding streets of Upper Brighton. Such were the houses built on Merseyside when these towns were growing rapidly and reaching maturity. There is little or no local character or identity about the houses and shops built since the end of the Second World War, so the character of these towns relies on the good husbandry of the owners of the older buildings.

On the whole, Wallasey was a very pleasant place to live for people who worked in the commerce and industry of Liverpool, just a ferry-ride away. Each township had its own shopping parades with characteristic iron and glass colonnades or canvas canopies over the footpaths, its own cinemas, recreation grounds and parks. Residents had ready access to beaches at Egremont, New Brighton and Wallasey.

There were altogether 12 cinemas in Wallasey in the 1950s, when the British film industry was at its zenith, and I went to all of them: the Embassy in Borough Road, the Marina in Brighton Street, the Queen's in Poulton Road, the Royal and Gaumont in King Street, the Continental in Liscard Road, the Capitol and Liscard Palace in Seaview Road, the Trocadero and Court in Victoria Road, the Winter Gardens in Atherton Street, and the Phoenix in Wallasey Village. As a boy I went to the pictures once or twice a week during the school holidays in the early 1950s, mainly at the Embassy and the Marina, which were the cheapest: 9d in the stalls and 1s 6d in the balcony.

The Embassy was the old Irving Theatre, the first in Wallasey to show films (news and documentaries), in 1904. Stan Laurel (then Stanley Jefferson) made his stage debut there in 1907. After a chequered history it was remodelled as a modern cinema in 1938. The Continental specialised in a repertoire of foreign films. The Winter Gardens was the largest and poshest cinema, with seating for 1,400; entertainment here alternated between live theatre and cinema. The Phoenix was a rare, post-war revival cinema, arising in 1951 from the ashes of the Coliseum, bombed in 1941. It was an ultra-modern, rectangular, flat-roofed building with an auditorium for 930 on one floor and two sound-proof rooms at the back with large windows and loudspeakers for parents with noisy children. Coffee and biscuits were served free in the interval. It survived till 1983.

Despite its wide streets and pleasant residential areas, Wallasey is a very compact, densely populated urban area with more than 90,000 people living in the townships on the plateau. The houses are packed close together and the front and back gardens are smaller than for similar houses of this quality in southern and eastern England. This – and the soot that spotted the washing on the line, darkened the roughcast and permeated indoors through shut windows on windy days – was a legacy of being part of an industrial conurbation with Birkenhead and Liverpool.

OPEN SPACES

This density of housing is offset by the liberal distribution of open spaces in parks, playing-fields,

recreation grounds, cemeteries and roadside landscaping. On the south side, a large tract of wasteland provided a buffer zone between the houses and the dockside mills, gas works and other industries, except in the southern extremities of Poulton and Seacombe, where houses faced oil storage tanks, engineering works or railway yards across the street.

In the built-up area of Wallasey most of the parkland has been acquired by the Council from the estates of early-18th-century mansions that once stood in open country, and some of these mansions still grace the parks. The 37-acre grounds of Liscard Hall were the nucleus of the 57-acre Central Park, the largest park in Wallasey, which forms a rural belt for 600-700 yards along the road between Seacombe and Liscard and an equally large open space between Egremont and Poulton. Liscard Hall itself is extant; in 1950 it was the School of Art. The grounds of Liscard Vale House and The Woodlands gave us the 25-acre Vale Park in Upper Brighton, sloping down the escarpment to the Mersey bank with views of ships and Bootle docks between the trees. Liscard Vale House is now the park café, office and store.

Earlston Gardens, also in Upper Brighton, were the gardens of Earlston House, now the Wallasey Central Library. The secluded Elleray Park in Hose Side Road at the back of New Brighton was the grounds of Elleray Park School, formerly Seafield House. The Grange, a peaceful oasis in Wallasey, was the garden of Wallasey Grange, now the clubhouse of the adjacent Municipal Golf Links; in the 1950s it was also a café. The park-like Wallasey Cemetery and the adjoining Earlston Gardens make a green break between Liscard and Upper Brighton.

Then there are the public open spaces that have been created out of disused quarries after the town had been built: Withens Lane Recreation Ground in Liscard, The Quarry in Upper Brighton, The Captain's Pit in Hose Side Road and The Breck in Wallasey. The Quarry is a cosy little park with a bowling green, hard tennis courts and a five-a-side football pitch, surrounded by gardens, deeply recessed in the bowels of the earth, hidden behind stone walls, well out of the wind, and can only be seen from the top of a bus. The Captain's Pit is a large fishpond enclosed in a small park. The Breck is the best of all the open spaces; it is the southern culmination of the western ridge and escarpment of the plateau and the last wilderness of ancient Wallasey, a tract of rock, heather and sand with isolated large blocks of harder sandstone, preserved as an informal adventure playground. It is just the place for 'Cowboys and Indians', and the only place in Wallasey where you can go rock-climbing.

Finally there are the incidental plantations alongside the roads and streets that give character to the townscape: the belts of gardens alongside Magazines Promenade, Upper Brighton, the public gardens around which St George's Park forms a secluded square near the top of New Brighton, the woodland plantations between the road and the houses on one side of Mount Road and Mount Pleasant Road at the back of New Brighton, and the floral roundabout in Grove Road, Wallasey, which is always a brilliant display of colour.

North of Wallasey the built-up area ends in an exhilarating expanse of grassy coastal dunes and wide open spaces overlooking the surf of the Irish Sea. The grass-covered sandhills are now the 44-acre Warren Municipal Golf Links and the adjoining 31-acre Harrison Park. The Warren, opened in 1909, was one of the first municipal links in Britain. Beyond lie the broad acres of open grassland reclaimed by the construction of King's Parade in 1935-39.

King's Parade was designed as a land reclamation scheme to build a grand new seafront that would have extended the resort from New Brighton to Wallasey and the start of a new road along the Wirral coast to the Dee. These open spaces were intended as sites for new hotels and flats fronting Coastal Drive, and sunken public gardens and other seaside amenities between Coastal Drive and King's Parade. War intervened and these designs were not fulfilled. Several fanciful schemes have since been mooted for the development of this area, but thankfully they have come to nothing. Any of these schemes would have been blighted by the demise of the British seaside holiday in the second half of the 20th century, and King's Parade would have been more of a 'white elephant' than it is. I think Wallaseyans prefer it as an informal, recreational open space. The borough council took away our natural heritage of cliffs, dunes and beach along this stretch of the coast; the least it can do is preserve this open space, which is one of the town's greatest amenities.

The grass-covered dunes that are now the Municipal Golf Links and Harrison Park were shifting sand dunes at the beginning of the 20th century. In 1906 the Royal Commission on Coast Erosion found that these dunes, once hundreds of yards wide, were narrowing at an alarming rate. Blown sand kept drifting over Harrison Drive, Wallasey, and the railway between Wallasey and New Brighton. This erosion was contained by a modest sea defence scheme of 1922-23, when a ramped embankment and walkway were built stretching half a mile east and 1¼ miles west of Harrison Drive. This stabilised the dunes and gave Wallasey its own seaside promenade, to which were added a colonnaded bathing station (1927 to 1940) and Derby Bathing Pool (1932 to 1984).

The bathing station provided a café and hire of costumes and towels. The commodious bathing pool, 110 yards by 25 yards, was the scene of swimming races. Local residents used Derby Bathing Pool, Guinea Gap Baths at Seacombe and the beaches at Egremont and Wallasey, while the visitors used the bathing pool and beach at New Brighton. Wallasey Beach is a bleak, windy spot and the tide goes out a long way across the flat sands. Bathers pitched hundreds of white tents on the beach in the 1930s. A few of us still pitched white tents on the beach in the 1950s.

The ramped sea wall of the Wallasey promenade did not form a channel along its foot to cut us off from the beach as does the King's Parade, and it left the cliffs and sands between Portland Street and Sea Road in their natural state. While it contained the erosion, it did not stop the nuisance of blown sand from the shore and the dunes, which still drifted over Harrison Drive and the railway. Corporation workmen had to sweep sand out of the tramlines in Warren Drive, and windborne sand even piled up in the lofts of houses on the heights of New Brighton.

The problem of drifting and windborne sand was one of the motives for the construction of the greater King's Parade, which has eclipsed 1 mile of the Wallasey promenade. Coastal Drive, running parallel with King's Parade, marks the alignment of the earlier promenade, which continues from a point 300 yards west of Harrison Drive as the sea wall today.

West of Wallasey lie the alluvial levels deposited by the tides that once made Wallasey an island. This land is the soil of the Wallasey Market Gardens, which in 1950 stretched for a mile west of Wallasey Village (on both sides of the railway) along a quarter-mile-wide strip between Leasowe Road and Green Lane in a neat chequerboard of square plots divided by high hedges to protect the crops from the sea winds. Wallasey was known for its market gardens, early potatoes and tomatoes. Seaward of the market gardens lie the Wallasey Golf Links, which, together with Leasowe Golf Links to the west, cover the site of the once famous Wallasey racecourse.

Above As smoke from the ferry and Mersey shipping drifts past in the background, the chiming clock on the **SEACOMBE BUS AND FERRY TERMINUS** tollhouse shows 12.15pm, and manual and clerical workers are coming off the ferry and making their way home after the routine Saturday half-day at work in 1950. Wallasey Corporation buses are lined up in herringbone order at the Portland stone loading colonnade in Victoria Place. The buses are scheduled to meet the ferry and are awaiting the 12.20 departure. Every 15 minutes – every 10 minutes in peak periods (including Saturdays) – the inspector's whistle blew, the cab doors slammed in quick succession and the buses left in convoy up Church Road, dispersing to all corners of the borough. (The second peak period on Saturday was from 12 noon to 2.00pm.) There were bays for 17 buses (including short-workings) on 10 routes here in Victoria Place, together with one for the Birkenhead joint service 12 around the corner in Birkenhead Road (off to the right). All 13 buses here were built in the period 1937 to 1948, 12 of them with Metropolitan Cammell bodies on Leyland chassis. The bus on route 4B at the right-hand end ran to Moreton (Bermuda Road) via Reeds Lane; this service was renumbered 5 in 1951.

The building behind the buses housed the ferry offices and a two-storey garage for 200 cars of ferry patrons. It also housed the bus inspector's office, a waiting room, a teetotal refreshment room and a confectionery kiosk. The ferry buildings and bus station, all in classical red brick and Portland stone, were rebuilt in 1930-33 to the design of the borough surveyor, Lionel Wilkinson, with gardens down the middle of Victoria Place and the spare bus rank on the left. The photograph is taken from the bottom of Church Road, still illuminated by gas, which was lit and extinguished by a lamplighter on a bicycle with a long pole and a hook to pull on the wire loops dangling from the valve lever at the top of the lamp. Street lights went off at midnight from the end of the war till the early 1970s. *The late George Greenwood*

Top right It was always ferry time in Wallasey, with 11 bus routes terminating at Seacombe and timed to meet the ferries. The buses unloaded at the ferry tollhouse (left) and passengers walked through the booking hall and straight on board the waiting ferry steamer. The grand 1930s classical tollhouse features a Portland stone frontage with an imposing central Romanesque arch, a bas relief carving of a galleon (from the borough coat of arms) on the keystone, and a colonnade of coupled Tuscan columns reminiscent of the Royal Naval

College at Greenwich. The colonnade continues around the corner of the forecourt to provide a covered walkway to the bus loading bays. Inside the booking hall are varnished Art Deco wooden booking offices and confectioner's and tobacconist's kiosks. Ferry tolls ranged from 3½d (children 2d) in 1950 to 6d (children 3d) in 1959. The peak year on Seacombe Ferry was 1920-21, when 21,932,176 passengers passed through the turnstiles. The post-war peak was 16,744,401 in 1947-48. The 1950s saw a steady decline from 15,926,297 in 1949-50 to 7,773,481 in 1959-60. As the buses unload their passengers the conductors had already turned the rear destination blinds for the return journeys: 1 to New Brighton via Seabank Road, 4 to Saughall Massie Hotel via Moreton Shore and 2 to Harrison Drive via Liscard. The buses seen here in 1954 (from left to right) were built in 1946, 1951 and 1952.

Above right After unloading at the ferry tollhouse (left), 1951 Wallasey bus No 44 takes its lay-over at the loading colonnade in evening sunshine during the summer of 1962 to await the arrival of the ferry before departing on route 17. This was the standard design of Wallasey bus for many years. The corporation took delivery of 130 buses with this style of bodywork by the Metropolitan Cammell Carriage & Wagon Company, Birmingham, between 1937 and 1951, mostly on Leyland chassis but some, in 1939, on AEC chassis. This bus, AHF 840, is one of the 1951 batch on Leyland Titan PD2 chassis that remained in service till 1970-73. There were detailed differences between each batch, half-drop windows giving way to sliding ventilators in the 1951 batch. The buses still carried the 'Wallasey Corporation Motors' legend on each side throughout the 1950s as they had done since the Leyland

Lions of 1926; the lettering was in gold leaf, outlined in black and shaded dark blue. The glorious 'primrose green' and cream livery remained clear of advertisements till declining revenue saw their advent in 1952. Wallasey's 'primrose green' was a creamy yellow with a slight tinge of green. Interior features of Wallasey buses were the French-polished mahogany window frames and beading in the saloons, and the Seacombe Ferry clock panel on the platform bulkhead showing the time of the ferry to Liverpool with which bus would connect when Seacombe-bound. (The sole survivor of the 130 classic Wallasey buses of this period, No 54 (AHF 850) of 1951, was preserved and restored by the author and is now in the borough transport museum at Taylor Street, Birkenhead.) Route 17 was the grand tour of the island, the longest route between Seacombe and New Brighton, via Poulton and Wallasey (5¼ miles against 2¾ miles by the direct route 1). It opened as tram route P (for Poulton) in 1910-11, was converted to motorbus in 1933 and closed in 1967.

Above Down the slope of this wide plain of granite setts in **VICTORIA PLACE, SEACOMBE**, where the incoming buses lumbered towards the river wall and the ferry tollhouse, we had this dramatic view across the gulf of the Mersey to the satanic mills of Liverpool towering and smoking in the background. This was the glimpse we had of Liverpool as the bus swung round the corner to the ferry tollhouse before we embarked on the ferry to the city of shipping offices. This was also the view from Seacombe Promenade, which began here, where we can glimpse five lads in short trousers by the railings. The spare bus rank was on the right, where older buses were stored between the peak periods, standing at right angles to the road with their backs to the gardens in the middle of the square. The satanic mills that form the backdrop to this view are specifically Tate & Lyle's sugar refinery at the end of Love Lane, Liverpool.

On the left of this 1954 view is a three-storey row of four late-Victorian shops with living quarters above. The two on the right, with the sturdy, iron colonnade, were built in 1880, and the two on the left, with the Dutch gables, terracotta ribbing and arched shop windows, were built in 1887. There were four shops here: from the left, W. E. McLachlan (tobacconist), with the Player's Navy Cut roundel on the gable, Mackie & Gladstone (wine and spirit merchants), Mrs Christina Jones (confectioner) and the Ferry Café. Beyond the shops the four-storey Seacombe Ferry Hotel took the bend into the promenade. Next to McLachlan's shop was the entrance to Seacombe Ferry Garage (motor engineers), which was behind the shops. The advertising hoardings on the left mask wasteland that was once the garden and bowling green of the former Regency double-bow-fronted Seacombe Hotel, which stood by the ferry slipway on the old river wall on a site now in the entrance of Birkenhead Road. The lower half of Victoria Place, the buildings in this picture and all the ferry premises are on 4 acres of land reclaimed in 1876-80 to fill in the bay in the river wall between the old Marine Parade and the North Reserve, the reclaimed land at the northern entrance of the docks. The old ferry slipway projected into the middle of this bay, south of the present ferry approach and landing place.

Below The London & North Eastern Railway, which served the eastern half of Britain, had four railheads on the west coast that were remote from the rest of the system: Seacombe (Cheshire), Southport (Lancashire), Silloth (Cumberland) and Mallaig

(Inverness-shire). The LNER did not own the lines into Seacombe or Southport (Lord Street), but worked the trains. **SEACOMBE & EGREMONT STATION**, seen here in 1952, was the northern terminus of services over an obscure triad of LNER lines inherited from the Great Central Railway, with trains from here and from Chester Northgate to Wrexham Central converging at Dee Marsh Junction. It was an anomalous enclave of LNER locomotives and varnished teak coaches in otherwise LMS and GWR territory.

The Seacombe line opened in 1895 as a branch of the Wirral Railway (Birkenhead to New Brighton and West Kirby), and in 1896 running powers over the branch were granted to the Great Central, whose line through mid-Wirral ended at Bidston. The branch remained in the ownership of the Wirral Railway and its successor, the LMS, which worked a service between Seacombe and West Kirby from 1895 till 1938. The Great Central was absorbed by the LNER in 1923 and from 1938 all Seacombe branch passenger trains were worked by that company.

This modest terminus on the Mersey bank, with an undulating wooden side platform, a concrete island platform, sparse corrugated-iron buildings and gas lighting, had its booking office at the top of Victoria Place. The terraced houses of Fell Street formed the backdrop beyond the coal sidings; these houses faced the railway, as the street was built on one side only. Trains left under Church Road

bridge (left). There were eight passenger trains a day to Connahs Quay and Wrexham Central in 1950. The last two coaches of this four-coach train are ex-Great Central, the nearest dating from 1904. The Seacombe branch closed to passengers in 1960 and to goods in 1963.

Top right Two ladies bend their backs into the climb up **FERRY VIEW ROAD, SEACOMBE**, which scales the low cliff as it leads us up from Seacombe Promenade to Mersey Street. The white lifebuoy, marked 'Wallasey County Borough', is hung in one of the dark green wooden stands that were placed at intervals along the inner side of the promenade from Seacombe to New Brighton. Iron bollards at the top of the slope bar access for motor vehicles to the promenade. We see the gable ends of terraces of houses fronting Seacombe Promenade, Denman Grove and Delamere Grove. The corner of the house on the left illustrates the practice of building with good-quality brick on the facade – in this case red Ruabon pressed brick – and cheaper brick on the sides and back, albeit offset with string courses and lintels of the better brick. Over the crest of the slope in this

1954 view we can see the hexagonal spirelet on the building at the corner of Borough Road and Demesne Street.

Above Viewed from Borough Road in 1954, the entrance to **MERSEY STREET, SEACOMBE**, was a grim scene with a bricked-up classical ruin on the left, the rough, pot-holed street paving, the lone gas lamp on a rusty iron post, the wasteland stretching to the right, and the backs of the terraced houses on Tudor Avenue sloping down to the river. It looks like a typical blitzed area of post-war Merseyside, but the wasteland, which stretched to Victoria Place, was not a bombed site; it had never been built on since it was abandoned as the gardens and bowling green of the early-19th-century Seacombe Hotel. The bricked-up ruin was the Seacombe branch of the North & South Wales Bank in the period 1885 to 1895 before it moved to a larger classical building further up Borough Road. This building then had a chequered career as a store, including, notably, Callow's cycles and guns, Wirral Furnishing Company and finally Ernest Downes, wholesale newsagent, before it was gutted in the air raids of 1941.

Above From the corner of Mersey Street (right) in 1954, this was the view up **BOROUGH ROAD, SEACOMBE**, the main street of Seacombe, as it led up the slope from the ferry into the town centre. This was originally Victoria Road, but was renamed Borough Road about 1918 to avoid confusion with Victoria Road, the main street of New Brighton. The picture shows the Borough Road frontage of the bricked-up classical bank/store that we saw in the last picture; this was No 14 Borough Road. Further along on the right are H. Dodds (shopfitter), Mrs Elizabeth Pearson's dining rooms, Abram Goldman (boot and shoe repairer) and Horace Green & Bertram (tobacconists). On the left, three Birkenhead Co-op coal lorries are lined up by Seacombe station coalyard, fully loaded ready for delivery, and the Queen's Arms public house stands on the corner of Fell Street.

Below The **LEASOWE CASTLE HOTEL, SEACOMBE**, the V-shaped corner tavern on the corner of Borough Road (centre) and Abbotsford Street (left), looked like something out of Liverpool dockland, but here the net curtains in the windows above are clean and white. On the right, the hexagonal spirelet we saw from Ferry View Road crowns the turret of the building on the V-shaped corner of Borough Road and Demesne Street (right). Courses of different-coloured tiles and bricks have been used on the spirelet and facades of this building. In 1954 the shops are, from the corner: Jack Bradley (wholesale confectioner and tobacconist), Stanley Weedon (hairdresser), James Manning (tobacconist and newsagent), then two empty shops; the one with the square clock dial is D. Freedman (furnisher). Next to Freedman's is the Griffin Hotel, then a bombed gap before the shops continue up Borough Road into the town centre. A 1940s Fordson van is parked in front of the empty shops.

Above At **SEACOMBE CROSSROADS** in 1954 the majestic Midland Bank (left), a classical building with a curved facade in red sandstone, and the ornate timber-framed clock tower (right) on the Five Bars Rest public house, dominate the junction of Church Road (foreground), Borough Road (right and left) and Brighton Street (background). Church Road and Brighton Street was the route most buses came from Seacombe Ferry to all parts of the borough, and the streets of Seacombe echoed to the guttural roar of post-war Leyland Titan buses. The Midland Bank was previously the North & South Wales Bank, which moved to these new premises in 1895 from the corner of Mersey Street. Turrets with spirelets were fashionable in late-Victorian and Edwardian Wallasey, and the square tower and spirelet on the Five

Bars Rest is balanced by the hexagonal one opposite on the Prudential Assurance office. Street lighting is in transition from gas to electric, and the pedestrian island was lit by an opaque white globular lamp on a tall post. An expensive 1939 Bentley car is parked on the right of Church Road, and a 1952 Fordson van stands at the foot of the long ladder on the left. This was the central crossroads of the old village of Seacombe, and the village pump once stood on the corner near the Bentley.

Above right In 1954 there was still pole-operated gas lighting along **BRIGHTON STREET, SEACOMBE**, the A554 road from New Brighton through the dingy reaches of Seacombe. The view is taken from the corner of Ellis Street (left) looking towards the ferry. Shops along the first block on the left-hand side were, from Ellis Street: James Mitty (tripe dresser), William Wearing (confectioner), J. Kenna (funeral director), Seacombe Post Office, and Frank Mellows (chemist). The Wallasey & Wirral Newspaper Company, publishers of the tabloid *Wallasey & Wirral Chronicle*, occupied the next block from Tabor Street to Shaw Street. Other side streets on the left were Chapel Street and Little Street. Shops on the right were: William Robinson (hairdresser), W. H. Carr (wallpaper merchant), Thomas Connor (tobacconist), John Logan (corn dealer), Mrs Helen Stuart (fruiterer), Charles Wood (furniture dealer) and Mrs Margaret Nuttall's on the corner of Victoria Grove. The drab red-brick streets of Seacombe were relieved by yellow-brick terraces in places and by chequered red and yellow brickwork, as seen above the shops on the left.

This page Wallasey's 4 miles of continuous promenade fronting the Mersey and the Irish Sea was what the 1949 New Brighton, Wallasey guide book (*below*) described as the 'grand stand of world shipping'. The walk along the **SEACOMBE PROMENADE** begins here at Seacombe Ferry. From the elevation of cliff-top gardens, we can see the U-shaped wake of the ferry steamer *Wallasey* or *Marlowe* of 1927 as it swings around into the ebb tide to berth at Seacombe Landing Stage on its three-quarter-mile passage from Liverpool. In the background a Canadian Pacific 'Empress' liner (left) and other ships are berthed along Liverpool Landing Stage in front of the Liver, Cunard and Dock offices.

Seacombe Promenade, built in 1901, is the south end of the Mersey bank promenade, 2½ miles long from Seacombe Ferry to New Brighton Pier. It is 21 feet above mean sea level, 45 feet wide and was surfaced, like the seaside promenade, as a normal road with an asphalt carriageway and a flagstone footpath with kerbs, ordinary street lamps and dark green railings atop the river wall. This was a true promenade, as all but the last 100 yards to New Brighton Pier was reserved for promenading only, being closed to all vehicles, including bicycles, except prams and Corporation service vehicles for maintenance. (It is still a pedestrian reservation today, flush-paved right across with the addition of a marked cycle path.) Although there were no vehicles, the orderly and well-dressed pedestrians of the period, all clad in their winter overcoats, still kept to the footpath. *Mason's Alpha series postcard*

SEACOMBE FERRY
THE RADAR CENTRE

LIVERPOOL WATERFRONT FROM SEACOMBE FERRY

Grand Stand of World Shipping To the inland dweller, New Brighton-Wallasey provides a fascination with which few resorts can enter into competition. The constant procession of ocean-going liners and thousands of other ships travelling parallel with the Promenades combine to create a lasting memory for the visitor, who may inspect the shipping at closer quarters by means of motor launch trips. A trip well worth while for the visitor is that to Liverpool Landing Stage by Ferry from New Brighton or Seacombe, and there board the Overhead Railway adjoining the Landing Stage which offers fine views of large ships at their berths. The great city of Liverpool itself also offers a pleasant day's outing to the visitor.

Trips by Sea Throughout the season, daily excursions leave Liverpool Landing Stage at 10.45 a.m. for Douglas, Isle of Man, and the North Wales resorts, Menai Bridge and Llandudno, arriving back in Liverpool at approximately 7.30 p.m.

River Cruises The River Cruises from Seacombe and New Brighton run by the Borough's world-famous ferry steamers have become well known throughout the country. Commodious and comfortable twin-screw vessels are employed, the latest type having three decks, including saloons and covered accommodation.

"THE DAFFODIL"
APPROACHING NEW BRIGHTON

Above right This was the view from North Seacombe Recreation Ground above the promenade, 300 yards south of the cliff-top site of Wallasey Town Hall. Arthur Mee wrote in *The King's England: Cheshire*: 'We know no town hall with a more splendid sight of a great city'. The impressive black Royal Liver Building dominates the scene with a Cunard liner and a Manx ferry berthed at Liverpool Landing Stage and freighters great and small moving up and down river. Wallaseyans in their hats and overcoats take the fresh, salty air along the promenade, joined by Liverpool visitors off the ferry taking this pleasant route to New Brighton. *Commercial postcard*

Right This picture can be titled **SEACOMBE AND EGREMONT** – the name of the railway station in Seacombe – because it shows parts of both townships. It was a three-quarter-mile walk from the station to the centre of Egremont along Brighton Street or the promenade. The left-hand side of the picture shows Seacombe Promenade and riverfront with Wallasey

Town Hall (centre) standing on the cliff top. The right-hand side shows Sandon Promenade, Egremont, and our viewpoint is the abutment in the river wall for Egremont Ferry tollhouse and pier.

Sandon Promenade is the oldest of the Wallasey promenades, built in 1891 from the foot of Sandon Road (centre) to Egremont Pier. The whole riverside promenade from Seacombe to New Brighton was completed by 1901; it had a rock-faced retaining wall of giant blocks of red sandstone with steps and slipways down to the sandy beaches. The promenade stabilised the eroding clay cliffs on which are built the villas facing the river in Egremont and Upper Brighton and the steep streets of houses that slope down to the river from Seacombe to New Brighton.

Wallasey Town Hall is an impressive, four-square, grey-stone, classical building with a central lantern tower; it faces the river with a broad flight of steps from Seacombe Promenade, but has its main entrance facing inland on Brighton Street. King George V laid the foundation stone in 1914 and the building was sufficiently complete by 1916 for it to be used as a military hospital during the First World War; it opened as a town hall in 1920. The interior is a grand, classical composition of grained white marble and oak panelling and pilasters. In the Second World War it was damaged by bombs in the air raids of 1940; the organ was wrecked but the building was restored. It was the seat of Wallasey County Borough Council till 1974 and is now the head office of Wirral Metropolitan Borough Council, governing the northern half of the peninsula. *St Albans series postcard*

Above The old **EGREMONT FERRY TOLLHOUSE** still stood on the abutment in the river wall where the pier once waded into the river. Egremont had a ferry service to Liverpool from 1830 till 1939. There is a record of a Liscard ferry in 1826 before Egremont got its name. This might have been the private ferry and landing place owned by Captain John Askew, Harbour Master of Liverpool and a local land-owner, who built himself a house that was later the ferry hotel, seen here half masked by the trees of the villa gardens sloping down the cliffs. He named his house Egremont after his native town in Cumberland, and the new township that sprang up around Church Street, athwart the manorial boundary of Seacombe and Liscard, also became known as Egremont.

Captain Askew began a public ferry service in 1830 with a short wooden pier, second-hand paddle-steamers and a high-water service only. He sold the ferry rights in 1835 to the Egremont Steam Ferry Company, which built a long, iron pier with a steam-powered 'run-out' extension and iron steamers. The ferry was taken over by Wallasey Local Board in 1861 and ferry steamers called at Egremont on the way between Liverpool and New Brighton. Under the aegis of Wallasey Borough Council, Egremont's second and last iron pier was a conventional one dating from 1909, with a bridge to a floating landing stage, replaced by a larger stage in 1929. The ferry service was suspended from 1932 to 1933 after the pierhead was wrecked by an oil tanker adrift from its anchorage. Winter service ended in 1936, then Egremont Pier and the ferry closed at the outbreak of war in 1939. A drifting coaster demolished the pier in 1941 and the stage was towed to South Tranmere shipbreakers; the ruined pier and the old slipway were removed in 1946-48. There was once a timber 'gridiron' and a crane this side of the ferry tollhouse for cleaning and repairing ferry steamers at low water. Since then ferries have been beached between Seacombe and Egremont for hull work. *St Albans series postcard*

Left A grim but romantic gloom hangs over the **EGREMONT FERRY HOTEL AND TOLLHOUSE** (right and left respectively) of the disused

Egremont Ferry, which once brought prosperity to this modest township on the Wallasey bank of the Mersey. Wind rattled the shutters on the tollhouse, which was the boathouse of the West Cheshire Sailing Club in the 1950s. The Egremont Ferry Hotel rounds off the corner from the slope of Tobin Street (right) to Sandon Promenade, its globular lantern nicely matching the curvature of the building. Through the gap, the grey silhouette of Seacombe Ferry Landing Stage can be seen jutting into the river three-quarters of a mile away, and the lone figure of a cloth-capped workman crests the brow of the street. The Ferry Hotel was the original Egremont, the house Captain John Askew built in 1823 with a garden sloping down to the shore. It was converted to a hotel by the Coulborn brothers after they bought the ferry company in 1849, becoming a free house named the Egremont Tap. Higson's Brewery of Liverpool bought it in 1901 and renamed it the Egremont Ferry Hotel.

The ferry tollhouse looked here, in 1954, much as it did when it was built in 1908-09; it closed to ferry passengers in 1939. A police telephone post stands on the footpath outside. Tobin Street is a short, steep climb to the town centre crossroads and the main shopping street. In ferry days this location at the junction of Tobin Street and the promenade was animated by crowds of Liverpool commuters, promenaders and families

going to the beach. In addition, from 1928 to 1938 Wallasey Corporation buses turned round in this space as Egremont Ferry was the terminus of a route to Albion Street, New Brighton, via Mount Road.

Top This Mersey-bank town was not advertised as a beach resort, but **EGREMONT BEACH** was firm and sandy, which, with the pleasant promenade, was the resort of Wallaseyans who shunned the crowds of visitors at New Brighton. A father and his two young boys enjoy the solitude, spaciousness, sunshine and silence, broken only by the estuary washing the shore, on this fine summer's morning. From the abutment for the old ferry pier and tollhouse, the red-rock-faced Egremont Promenade, built in 1891, stretches towards New Brighton, backed by the bosky gardens of villas facing the river. The clock tower in the middle distance marks Cliff House (1882), the central building of the Liverpool Home for Aged Mariners in its 5-acre park, with cottages, apartment villas and bungalows in the grounds of the former Liscard Manor House between Maddock Road and Manor Lane. The mariners' homes were founded by William Cliff, a Liverpool merchant, and are run by the Mercantile Marine Service Association for retired ships' officers, their wives and widows. The 135-foot clock tower was demolished with

Cliff House in 1981. Beyond the mariners' homes we can see the trees of Vale Park in Upper Brighton and the Tower Building and pier at New Brighton on the corner of the Mersey estuary and the Irish Sea. The townships of Egremont, Upper Brighton and New Brighton were built in the manor and civil parish of Liscard, and the northern part of Egremont from Trafalgar Road to Holland Road was still regarded as Liscard in the early 20th century. *St Albans series postcard*

Above This was the grandstand view the ancient mariners had of shipping in one of the world's busiest ports. This photograph of **EGREMONT PROMENADE** was taken from the gardens of the Mariners' Homes on the stretch of promenade just north of Maddock Road slipway (pictured) in spring morning sunshine. Gas lamps lit the way by night. The grey silhouettes of Liverpool waterfront and Seacombe Steamboat Station are along the horizon. The tide is low, exposing a stretch of sand and stones – time to take the dog for a walk along the empty beach. This was a continuation of Wallasey's Mersey-bank promenade from Seacombe to New Brighton, a pleasant, interesting walk without the noise of motor traffic or seaside amusements, backed by the sloping gardens of villas facing the river. *Mason's Alpha series postcard*

Above **MOTHER REDCAP'S, EGREMONT**, was the most historic house in Wallasey. Behind a rock-faced red sandstone wall and arched gateway on Egremont Promenade, between Lincoln Drive and Caithness Drive, stood this remarkable Victorian villa with ornate timberwork and a spired lookout turret, latterly Mother Redcap's Café. The dates on the window lintel under the front gable, 1595 and 1889, tell us that the house is much older than it looks. It was rebuilt and enlarged in 1889 around the original two-storey stone house of 1595, which was only approached along the shore of the trackless wastes of Liscard Moor or from ships anchoring in Red Bet's Pool. A stone wall retained the banked front garden against high water. In the 18th century the house became an inn, patronised by merchant sailors, smugglers, privateers, fishermen and river pilots. It had its own brewhouse at the back, a well fed by a beck off Liscard Moor, cellars, trapdoors, hiding places and tunnels leading inland from the well shaft and yard cellar. This cellar stored contraband rum, salt, sugar and tobacco, then heavily taxed, and was camouflaged with beams, flagstones and heaps of manure and coal, landed in Red Bet's Pool, to supply Liscard and Wallasey villages. A dummy windvane on a flagstaff outside the tavern pointed away from the house or towards the house as an indication to smugglers and sailors whether the coast was clear of excisemen and the press gang.

The most famous licensee was widow Polly Jones, known as Mother Redcap, from about 1780. She boarded merchant sailors hiding from the press gang for privateers while their ships were berthed in Liverpool, and banked their money in hiding places while they were at sea. She died in her 80s, and in 1862 the inn reverted to a private house. Joseph Kitchingman remodelled the house in 1889 and gave part of the front garden for the construction of Egremont Promenade in 1891, on condition that it should not be a public carriageway. Thanks to him the whole promenade from Seacombe to New Brighton is still traffic-free today. Photographed in 1954, the long-empty, derelict house was demolished 20 years later. A verse on Mother Redcap's inn sign began 'All ye that are weary come in and take rest'. Today it is the site of Mother Redcap's Nursing Home.

Above right **LISCARD ROAD, EGREMONT**, leading from Seacombe to Liscard, bends through this shady nook at the back of Egremont marked by the King's Arms Hotel and a terrace of four Georgian houses. The trees on the left of this 1973 view mark the eastern corner of Central Park, 57 acres, which borders the road for 700 yards to the built-up area of Liscard. The King's Arms was built in 1932 on the corner of narrow Church Lane to replace an earlier hotel of the same name on this side of the lane end. The four late-Georgian, or Regency, houses are 78 to 84 Liscard Road, comprising Littler's Terrace, one of the earliest urban housing developments in rural Wallasey. Beyond the terrace, on the corner of Church Street, was Mrs Hilda Amey's Central Kiosk selling newspapers, tobacco and sweets. The Grecian parish church of St John, Egremont, is just around the bend, standing in an enclave of the park fronting Liscard Road and facing down Church Street, the main axis of mid-19th century Egremont, to the town centre, Tobin Street and the ferry.

Below **LITTLER'S TERRACE, EGREMONT,** comprised some of the earliest terraced houses of urban Wallasey, contemporary with the Georgian houses in Martin's Lane, Liscard, and predated only by isolated red sandstone cottages of the island's rural era. Shown here in 1973 are Nos 80 to 84 Liscard Road. They were built in the prevailing late-Georgian or Regency style as gentlemen's houses overlooking Central Park in the formative days of the township of Egremont, probably about the time of the classical parish church (1832-33), almost opposite, on the edge of the park. They are built in

old Cheshire brindled brickwork – brown, red and yellow – featuring round-headed doorways with columns and fanlights, sash windows with sandstone sills and lintels, and a sandstone parapet fronting a low-pitched roof. No 84 (left) has been partly refaced in different brick. With the decline of Egremont since the 1930s, these houses have fallen on harder times and are not listed buildings with planning protection by the borough council, but they survive as a brief glimpse of an earlier civilisation in the otherwise late-Victorian and Edwardian frontages of Liscard Road.

Above The oldest house in Wallasey, rock solid in local sandstone with small mullioned windows, stands on the left at the wide north end of **LIMEKILN LANE, POULTON**, on the corner of Poulton Bridge Road. The datestone can be variously read as 1621, 1627, 1691 or 1697, as the last two digits are ambiguous. It is known simply as the Old House, but is generally called Bird's House after the Bird family who built it and lived there for many years. It later became the ancestral home of the Woosnam family, and William Woosnam was living there at the time of this 1954 photograph. The stone barn on the extreme left is dated 1704. The house and barn are preserved unaltered by the National Trust.

The township of Poulton is named after Wallasey Pool; it stood at the head of the creek and was a natural harbour most conveniently sited for the neighbouring villages of Liscard and Wallasey, both within a mile, when land access via Leasowe and transport by road were arduous. In the 16th and 17th centuries Poulton rivalled the ports of Chester and Liverpool, with a greater tonnage of shipping. In this scene, Poulton Bridge Road sweeps down the slope of Wallasey Pool to the swing bridge across the docks built along the old creek. The Old House is grimy with the smoke of dockland. Ranks of molasses storage tanks along Dock Road march incongruously right up to the Old House on the lower side, the wharves of the West Float and Bidston Dock are only 200 yards from this corner, and from 1955 there came the dust and din of the giant iron-ore cranes then erected on Bidston Dock. Three labourers in cloth caps and boots amble across Limekiln Lane back towards dockland after lunch. Cottages line the other side of Poulton Bridge Road, with Mrs Hilda Panton's newsagent's shop (the former Post Office) on the corner. St Luke's Church, built in 1899-1900, crowns the scene, standing at the crossroads in the centre of Poulton.

Below **MILL LANE, POULTON**, sweeps down the southern slope of Wallasey plateau from Liscard to St Luke's Church, silhouetted against the noonday sun in 1954. On its descent the lane spanned the narrow rock gorge carrying the railway branch line to Seacombe under the bridge by the first telegraph pole and the advertising hoardings. Liscard & Poulton station huddled in

the shady cutting to the right of the bridge, approached by a ramp with access between the bridge and the turreted corner of Station Road (left). Rostherne Avenue runs off to the left along the north brink of the railway cutting. Shops up the slope of Mill Lane from the corner of Station Road are John Holden (newsagent and tobacconist), Grayson & Martin (piano repairers), Thomas Shakespeare (engineer), Leslie Crockford (hardware dealer), Mrs Margaret Dickinson (who is seen standing on the doorstep of her fried fish shop), and Mrs Ann Gordon (draper). Above the shop windows the buildings are faced in yellow brick trimmed with red-brick architraves, string courses and cornices.

Mill Lane is named after a former corn mill, a wooden post mill, the earliest kind of windmill, shown on a map of 1665 standing on the hill just west of St Luke's Church, up Breck Road. The name still has significance: the descent of the lane from Woodstock Road gives a distant prospect of Bidston Mill, a preserved brick tower mill with sails, in a direct line ahead on top of Bidston Hill, the next ridge to the south-west. This vista was best seen from the top of a bus as it swayed down Mill Lane on route 17 to Seacombe, route 9 to Charing Cross or route 18 to Woodchurch.

Top right Lying in the red-rock cutting west of Mill Lane bridge, **LISCARD & POULTON STATION**, pictured in 1951, had an island platform with a single track each side and a coal siding at the foot of the stone-walled access ramp on the left. The up line is masked by the grassy top of the cutting in the foreground and the down line is hidden behind the platform. Passengers walked from the ramp through the covered wooden footbridge and staircase down to the platform. The station was in Poulton, three-quarters of a mile from the centre of Liscard via Liscard Road and Mill Lane. The Seacombe branch and its two stations were built by the Wirral Railway in 1895, passing to the LMS in 1923; trains from Seacombe ran to West Kirby from 1895 till 1938. From 1896 the line was also used with running powers by the GCR (later part of the LNER) with trains to Connahs Quay and Wrexham Central, and from 1938 onward the line was worked entirely by the LNER till nationalisation in 1948. Trains continued to run from Seacombe to Wrexham with ex-GCR/LNER engines and carriages till the line closed to passengers in 1960; coal and goods traffic ended in 1963. The red-brick gable ends of the terraced houses in Killarney Grove on the cliff top are decorated with patterns in yellow brick, while their fronts are faced in yellow brick variegated with red-brick string courses and architraves.

Above The south-facing seat was ideal for a siesta in the noon sunshine during the long wait between trains in this quiet station in the shelter of the cutting, which also cut out much of the sound of the outside world. The warmth of the August sun in 1954 is reflected off the red sandstone cutting and the rubblestone wall of the ramp road to the coalyard. The peace is broken only by the occasional sound of shovelling coal from the trucks on the siding into hundredweight sacks on a coal merchant's lorry at the foot of the ramp behind us, and by the occasional hollow-sounding tread of a passenger over the knobbly, knotted floorboards of the covered wooden footbridge and down the staircase. The footbridge, staircase, station offices and platform were lit by dim, mumbling gas lamps after dark. Despite the torpid train service, the faint odour of soot hangs in the air. We are standing on the down platform looking along the line towards Seacombe. How many people waited on this platform to board the eight trains a day for the 1½-mile journey to Seacombe? From St Luke's Church there were ten buses an hour on routes 3, 4, 5 and 17 in the off-peak and 18 buses an hour in the peak, plus shortworkings.

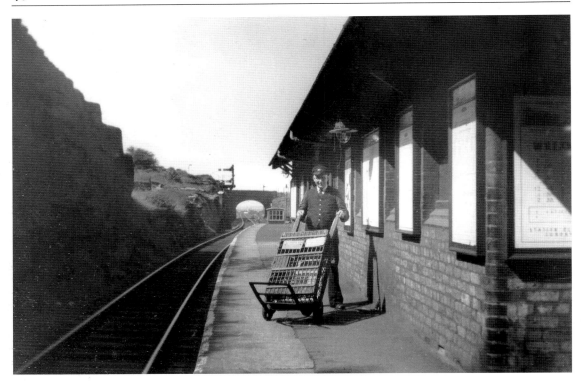

This page George, the friendly porter, booking clerk and general factotum at **LISCARD & POULTON STATION**, poses for this 1954 photograph with his luggage trolley of empty racing pigeon baskets on the up platform under one of the gas lamps with its trailing wires for lighting-up and snuffing-out. The eaves of the station roof are extended to form a scanty canopy that afforded little or no shelter from the rain on a windy day. This photograph is similar to a picture postcard that was on sale all over Britain in Edwardian times showing a railway porter with a woman sitting on his luggage trolley and the words 'A lively load' – the photograph was taken here on this platform. The cabin at the end of the platform houses a ground frame that controls the points for the coal siding. The signals were controlled from Slopes Branch signal cabin (named after a former villa called Slopes) just beyond Breck Road bridge. That cabin also controlled Slopes Branch Junction, where the branch line of that name sloped down a bank of wasteland and led alongside Dock Road to Seacombe. The up line headed west across fens to Bidston, then south through the vale of mid-Wirral to Dee Marsh Junction (for Chester) and a long, steady climb uphill to Wrexham Central.

In 1950 there were eight trains a day between Seacombe and Wrexham, nine on Saturdays and three on Sundays. There were also three shortworkings to and from Connahs Quay & Shotton serving Shotton steelworks at Hawarden Bridge Halt on the River Dee. You climbed into a vintage GCR or LNER compartment carriage and sat down in a cloud of dust and soot exhaled from the thick seat cushions. The train stopped at all stations on the way, some with charming names such as Heswall Hills, Burton Point for Burton & Puddington and Caergwrle Castle & Wells. The 30-mile journey took about an hour and a half, an average speed of 20mph.

Above right Standing in the north-west corner of this four-way road junction, the **PRIMROSE HOTEL, LISCARD**, is a picturesque Cheshire-style building in red sandstone with mullioned windows, a gabled porch like a church and an applied timber framework on the upper elevation. The hotel was built about 1860 and the decorative timberwork was added in 1923. It stands at the south end of Withens Lane, which runs north past St Mary's Church (1876-77) towards Upper Brighton. Shops mark the corner of Greenwood Lane (formerly Green Lane, right) leading to Egremont. Martin's Lane, with its late-Georgian houses, leads off to the left to

PLEASE RETAIN THIS BILL FOR REFERENCE   f 220-R (Day)

EXCURSIONS
(FIRST & THIRD CLASS)

EACH WEEKDAY
30th June to 13th September (incl.) 1952
TO

Caergwrle Castle
AND
Wrexham

FROM		TIMES OF DEPARTURE		RETURN FARES (Third Class)	
				Caergwrle Castle	Wrexham
		a m	a m	a m	s d	s d
Seacombe & Egremont	"A"	9 38	11 28	2 30	3 6	4 6
Liscard & Poulton		9 41	11 31	2 33	3 5	4 6
Bidston		9 46	11 36	2 39	4 9	5 9
Upton		9 50	11 40	2 44	4 6	5 6
Heswall Hills		9 59	11 49	2 53	3 6	4 6
Neston & Parkgate	"B"	10 6	11 56	3 0	3 0	3 11
Burton Point	"B"	10 10	12 0	3 4	2 6	3 6
		p m				
Caergwrle Castle	arr.	10 45	12*39	3 40	*Arrives 5 minutes later on Saturdays
Wrexham (Central)		11 5	12*54	3 56	

A—Bookings to Caergwrle apply by any train.
B—Bookings to Wrexham apply by any train.

RETURN ARRANGEMENTS
Passengers return same day from WREXHAM (Central) or CAERGWRLE CASTLE by any train.

First Class Tickets will be issued at proportionate fares (fractions of 3d. reckoned as 3d.)

Owing to Passenger Train Alterations during August Bank Holiday period, passengers are requested to verify the train services shown hereon, as they may be amended.

TICKETS CAN BE OBTAINED IN ADVANCE AT STATIONS AND AGENCIES
Further information will be supplied on application to Stations, Agencies, or to T. C. BYROM, District Passenger Superintendent, Lime Street Station, Liverpool. Tel. No. ROYal 4292 (Ext. 40.)

Central Park and Liscard shops. This 1954 view is taken from the north end of Serpentine Road. A pale-blue police telephone post stands on the right-hand corner, which was still undeveloped, while a 1949 Morris Oxford car makes a right turn from Greenwood Lane into Withens Lane.

Below Viewed from the roundabout in the centre of Liscard, a 1946 Wallasey Corporation bus wends its way through the narrow, crowded shopping street of **LISCARD ROAD** southbound on route 14 from New Brighton to Seacombe. This was the unprepossessing main shopping street in Wallasey. The trees of Central Park can be glimpsed at the end of the shops on the right, and there the road widened out to a pleasant aspect on its way to Egremont and Seacombe. Shops on the left are F. W. Woolworth's bazaar, built in 1930, James Coombes (boot repairer), Johnson Brothers (dyers and cleaners), Finlason (optician), Boots (chemists) and W. Lawn (fishmonger). From the right are Harold Williams (men's outfitters), Mansfield (shoes), Joseph Bennett (grocer), the National Provincial Bank, Marks & Spencer and Sayer (bakers). The two cars in the foreground are Wallasey-registered DHF 4, a 1955 Vauxhall Wyvern (left), and DHF 619, a 1956 Morris Minor Traveller (right), an estate car with a wooden frame at the back. *Commercial postcard*

Above Electricity House of 1934 (right) and Coronation Buildings of 1937 (left) dominate the Liscard end of **WALLASEY ROAD, LISCARD**, giving a 1930s modernist flavour of white and cream faced buildings of steel and concrete construction with flat roofs to this wide shopping street, and continuing the theme of inter-war architecture that we have already seen in the Capitol cinema (1926), Woolworth's bazaar (1930) and the Wellington Hotel (1937), which are key buildings in the townscape here. Electricity House fills the block between St Alban's Terrace and Conway Street. It was built by Wallasey Municipal Electricity Department, which had its own generating stations from 1897 till 1934, when the power station at the bottom of Limekiln Lane, Poulton, was taken over by the Central Electricity Board, but Wallasey Corporation was still responsible for distribution and service. From nationalisation of the industry in 1948, Electricity House was the Wallasey district office of the Merseyside & North Wales Electricity Board. It housed clerical and technical staff, a showroom and a theatre for cookery and other demonstrations.

Coronation Buildings was a typical mid-1930s parade of shops with horizontal metal windows and a parapet, adjoining the Wellington Hotel of the same date at the far end, where black and white bollards on a zebra crossing island mark the approach to the roundabout at the central crossroads of Liscard. A 1948 Wallasey Corporation bus on route 2 from Seacombe to Harrison Drive stops to load a queue at Burton's corner of Liscard Road. The building behind it is Martin's Bank (1908), a characteristic Edwardian-baroque bank in red brick and Portland stone on the corner of Liscard Road and Liscard Village, the former village street, in the background. The wide carriageway has no road markings except for the bus stops, and the only moving vehicle in this 1954 photograph is a bicycle. A

1953 Morris Minor car is parked outside Coronation Buildings, and a 1933 Wolseley outside the Castle Hotel on the right. The self-standing delivery bicycle (left) still has its wartime blackout white band on the back mudguard.

Above right The **BOOT INN, LISCARD**, a large, handsome, neo-Tudor public house of 1924, stands on the reverse curves of Wallasey Road where it crosses the township boundary into Wallasey, which lies just around the second bend, beyond the tree. The first Boot Inn, a thatched cottage, was one of four inns on Wallasey island in the 16th century, the others being the Seacombe Boat House, the Pool Inn at Poulton and the Cheshire Cheese in Wallasey village. The legend of the boot is that in the late 16th century a fierce, bloodstained highwayman carrying a pistol and a jackboot roused the innkeeper in the middle of the night, demanding meat and ale. There was the clink of gold as the stranger thumped the jackboot on the table. While plying him with food and drink the innkeeper seized the pistol and had the robber bound by his wife and daughter. They restored the gold to a man who arrived shortly afterwards with a bloody head and a missing boot. He rewarded the hosts with 20 guineas and gave his boot to be the sign of the inn. The robber was hanged. The jackboot is preserved in a glass case on display at the inn. The second Boot Inn, a two-storey stone building, stood in what is now the middle of the road and was demolished for road widening in 1925 after the new inn was built behind it on the corner of Newton Road (off to the left). The entrance of Cecil Road is in the left foreground of this 1954 view by the Belisha beacon marking the zebra crossing. Propped up by the kerb is a motorised delivery bicycle, a heavy machine with a carrier on the front and a petrol engine on the back.

Below Gas still lit the way from Liscard to New Brighton in 1954, and this short lamp post on the corner of **RAKE LANE, LISCARD** (left), and Edinburgh Road (right) was standard along many main roads in Wallasey well into the 1950s. The cast-iron post, with its graceful concave base, was the same as we see in Edwardian postcards of Wallasey with rectangular lanterns, which were later replaced by these swan-neck brackets with semi-globular, pendant lanterns. The lights here were switched on and off by time-switches instead of a lamplighter's pole-hook; they came on at dusk and went off at midnight until the early 1970s. Wallasey had its own gas works off Dock Road,

Poulton, from 1860. The municipal gas undertaking was taken over by the National Gas Board in 1949. The Queen's Arms stands at the focal point at the lower end of the road, where it bends to the right into Liscard Village, a street name defining the short extent of the former one-street village of Liscard. Some stone cottages survive in the entrance of Manor Road. The Queen's Arms was the terminus of the only Crosville country bus service into Wallasey, the 106 from West Kirby, running every 20 minutes via Meols, Moreton and Leasowe. The service began in 1920 to Wallasey Village, was extended to Liscard Village in 1925 and ended (as service F34) in 1979.

Above **RAKE LANE, UPPER BRIGHTON**, leads from Liscard to Upper Brighton on the road to New Brighton ('rake' is from an Old Norse word found in Wirral meaning a path, cattle drove or pasture). The Edwardian houses on the left are built in a vernacular style indigenous to the Mersey-bank towns from New Ferry to New Brighton. Halsbury Road is the side street on the left. The Wallasey bus on route 14 waits at the black and white signal posts at the crossing of Penkett Road (right) and Earlston Road (left). (There are no signals at this crossroads today.) Bus route 14 replaced the former RL (Rake Lane) tram route in 1933, following the same course all the way from New Brighton to Seacombe via Liscard. The trees on the right beyond the bus in this 1954 view are in Sandheys Park, home ground of New Brighton Football & Athletic Club

(called 'The Rakers') from 1921 to 1944, then the site of a 'prefab' housing estate. New Brighton FC played in the Third Division North of the Football League from 1923 to 1951, and before the war they entertained Sheffield Wednesday, Stoke City, Tottenham Hotspur and Wolverhampton Wanderers in FA Cup ties at Sandheys Park. Wallasey Corporation was economical with its street lighting here, with one short bracket lamp on the right and another suspended from a span wire at the crossroads. The main street of Upper Brighton lies just ahead, around the bend.

Below left This is Rowson Street, the main street of Upper Brighton, a short thoroughfare of shops and houses on the hilltop above New Brighton on the road from Liscard. At the other end, Rowson Street begins the descent into New Brighton. On the right is the **LITTLE BRIGHTON INN, UPPER BRIGHTON**, built about 1845 as the Chequers. In 1849 it was renamed the Jenny Lind after the Swedish opera singer, Johanna Lind, who stayed there while appearing in Liverpool in 1848. It has been the Little Brighton Inn since

1855, named after Little Brighton Common opposite, which was an area of heathland left wild for quarrying stone in the 19th century. Little Brighton was the earlier name of Upper Brighton.

Beyond the inn in 1954 we see the shops of Mrs Jessie Peck (newsagent), John Heald (cabinet-maker), George Reader (grocer), Charles Seddon (florist), John Irwin (grocer) and John Vaughan (newsagent) up to the corner of Manville Road. A man in a white coat unloads a delivery for George Reader from a blue and white van of Hunter's cooked meats, of Liverpool. The trees on the left stand behind the wall of the bowling green in the former quarry of Little Brighton Common, which provided the stone for the Little Brighton Inn. The building with the lantern next to the bowling green is the Sandridge Hotel, built in the early 1870s.

Top On **ROWSON STREET, UPPER BRIGHTON**, in 1954, at the top of the climb out of New Brighton, a Wallasey bus pauses at the iron stop flag on the gas lamp post opposite the Technical School of 1901, with its prominent cupola, in Field Road. Over the brow, Rowson Street becomes the main street of Upper Brighton, and we can see the garage of H. A. Turner, the undertaker; the words 'Motors for weddings, cars for hire' are moulded in the concrete fascia above the garage portal. The bus, a 1952 Weymann-bodied Leyland, shows the full route details on the back as on the front, which was the tradition in Wallasey and Birkenhead. The red-on-white destination in the upper screen indicates that it is on a short working of route 14 to Lloyd's Corner in Seacombe. This location was the 'New

Brighton' terminus – just over half a mile short of New Brighton Pier – of Wallasey's 2¾-mile single-line horse tramway from Seacombe Ferry via Brighton Street, Liscard Road and Rake Lane from 1879 to 1901: the descent into New Brighton was too steep for horse-drawn vehicles. The grey sandstone house on the left was the backdrop of old photographs of the horse trams, and a line forked off (right) to the tram sheds and stables in Field Road, which survived into the early 1990s as a motorcar workshop.

Above **SEABANK ROAD, UPPER BRIGHTON**, runs along the top of the cliffs from Egremont to Upper Brighton, with steep streets of large houses running down to the river (to the right). The northern reach of Seabank Road arrives in the pleasant Edwardian residential area of Upper Brighton, where the domestic architecture features facades of grey pebble-dash above Ruabon pressed red brick with decorative timber-framing, battlements, corner towers, turrets and spirelets, even on moderate-sized terraced and semi-detached houses. The houses on the left are terraced, with Ormiston Road and Onslow Road in between. The former tramway traction poles, minus their ornamental scrollwork, have been adapted for street lighting. The primrose-and-cream Wallasey bus on the horizon of this 1954 view, 'like a ray of sunshine coming along the road', is on route 1, the direct route from New Brighton to Seacombe. This route was formerly line S (for Seabank Road), the first Wallasey tramway to be replaced by a bus service, in 1929.

Above These two remarkable buildings – the **ROUND-HOUSE AND BATTERY, UPPER BRIGHTON** – face each other across the junction of Magazine Lane (left) and Magazine Brow (right), viewed here in 1954 from Fort Road, with the trees of Vale Park in the background. The Roundhouse (left) with its conical roof, was built in 1839 for the watchman of the powder magazines sited here; ships left their gunpowder here while in port, all merchant ships being armed in those days. The magazines dated from about 1765, when this was an uninhabited area of heath and dunes north of Liscard. The powder was stored in bunkers in a walled compound. New Brighton and Upper Brighton developed from the early 1830s and the magazines were removed in 1851 to hulks moored up-river off Eastham; the houses of Aylesbury Road and Lichfield Road stand on the site today.

Liscard Battery, as it was known then, was built in 1858 as a second line of defence of the Mersey entrance after Fort Perch Rock of 1829. Soldiers were garrisoned here, but its guns were never fired. The battery was sold to Liverpool Yacht Club in 1912 and its walls, 90 yards by 60 yards, now enclose two pairs of semi-detached houses, flanked by two detached houses and their gardens, built between the two world wars. A smartly dressed couple take their baby out in an elegant high pram to the park and the promenade.

Above right The 25-acre **VALE PARK, UPPER BRIGHTON**, slopes down the Mersey bank to the riverside promenade. A dredger and a coaster ride at anchor offshore, neatly filling the two defiles in the tree canopy. The backdrop of Liverpool's northern dockland at Kirkdale and Bootle is in stark contrast to the Cheshire bank of the river at this point. This 1961 view across the river is of dock walls, ships in dock, derricks, cranes, transit sheds and warehouses, with chimney stacks and church spires on the skyline into the distance. Vale Park is one of the

attractions of New Brighton, the seaside resort neighbour of Upper Brighton, being a pleasant 700 yards' walk along the promenade from New Brighton Pier (see next picture), but its amenities and band concerts are probably enjoyed more by the local population than visitors to the resort. It opened as a public park in 1899 in the former grounds of two mansions, Liscard Vale House (left), which became a park café, office and store, and The Woodlands (nearer Vaughan Road), which was demolished in 1910. The classical domed bandstand was built in 1926 and the arena of deckchairs on the uphill side of it has been filled by audiences for concerts by all the famous mill-town brass bands, lesser-known bands, marionette shows and local talent shows. In the 1950s the floral clock was another feature of the park; it was sited (left of centre) on the railed-off slope in front of the house facing the bandstand.

Right **MAGAZINES PROMENADE, UPPER BRIGHTON**, is the most pleasant stretch of the 2½-mile walk along the 45-foot-wide traffic-free promenade from Seacombe to New Brighton. There are 700 yards to go to New Brighton Pier and the ferry landing stage, glimpsed on the right, at the very mouth of the Mersey. In this 1954 view we are abreast of Vale Park, and the dwarf wall and high railings along the front of the park are lined with elegant Edwardian benches along the inner footpath of the promenade. The seats continue along the belt of trees and gardens stretching north from Vale Park in front of the ornate Edwardian houses of Oakland Vale, with their turrets and spirelets, facing the river. Our approach to New Brighton is indicated by the coloured illuminations strung along the tops of the ornate cast-iron lamp posts. The trees do not end in the middle of this picture but continue around the bend in the promenade where Magazines Promenade, Upper Brighton, gives way to Tower Promenade, New Brighton. Both promenades opened in 1899.

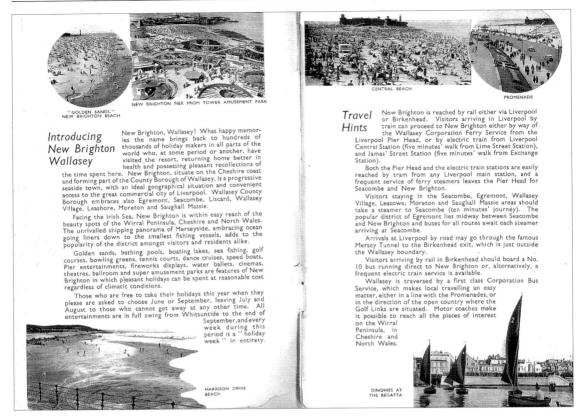

"GOLDEN SANDS,"
NEW BRIGHTON BEACH

NEW BRIGHTON PIER FROM TOWER AMUSEMENT PARK

CENTRAL BEACH

PROMENADE

Introducing New Brighton Wallasey

New Brighton, Wallasey! What happy memories the name brings back to hundreds of thousands of holiday makers in all parts of the world who, at some period or another, have visited the resort, returning home better in health and possessing pleasant recollections of the time spent here. New Brighton, situate on the Cheshire coast and forming part of the County Borough of Wallasey, is a progressive seaside town, with an ideal geographical situation and convenient access to the great commercial city of Liverpool. Wallasey County Borough embraces also Egremont, Seacombe, Liscard, Wallasey Village, Leashore, Moreton and Saughall Massie.

Facing the Irish Sea, New Brighton is within easy reach of the beauty spots of the Wirral Peninsula, Cheshire and North Wales. The unrivalled shipping panorama of Merseyside, embracing ocean going liners down to the smallest fishing vessels, adds to the popularity of the district amongst visitors and residents alike.

Golden sands, bathing pools, boating lakes, sea fishing, golf courses, bowling greens, tennis courts, dance cruises, speed boats, Pier entertainments, fireworks displays, water ballets, cinemas, theatres, ballroom and super amusement parks are features of New Brighton in which pleasant holidays can be spent at reasonable cost regardless of climatic conditions.

Those who are free to take their holidays this year when they please are asked to choose June or September, leaving July and August to those who cannot get away at any other time. All entertainments are in full swing from Whitsuntide to the end of September, and every week during this period is a " holiday week " in entirety.

Travel Hints

New Brighton is reached by rail either via Liverpool or Birkenhead. Visitors arriving in Liverpool by train can proceed to New Brighton either by way of the Wallasey Corporation Ferry Service from the Liverpool Pier Head, or by electric train from Liverpool Central Station (five minutes' walk from Lime Street Station), and James' Street Station (five minutes' walk from Exchange Station).

Both the Pier Head and the electric train stations are easily reached by tram from any Liverpool main station, and a frequent service of ferry steamers leaves the Pier Head for Seacombe and New Brighton.

Visitors staying in the Seacombe, Egremont, Wallasey Village, Leasowe, Moreton and Saughall Massie areas should take a steamer to Seacombe (ten minutes' journey). The popular district of Egremont lies midway between Seacombe and New Brighton and buses for all routes await each steamer arriving at Seacombe.

Arrivals at Liverpool by road may go through the famous Mersey Tunnel to the Birkenhead exit, which is just outside the Wallasey boundary.

Visitors arriving by rail in Birkenhead should board a No. 10 bus running direct to New Brighton or, alternatively, a frequent electric train service is available.

Wallasey is traversed by a first class Corporation Bus Service, which makes local travelling an easy matter, either in a line with the Promenades, or in the direction of the open country where the Golf Links are situated. Motor coaches make it possible to reach all the places of interest on the Wirral Peninsula, in Cheshire and North Wales.

HARRISON DRIVE
BEACH

DINGHIES AT
THE REGATTA

Above Pages from the 1949 New Brighton, Wallasey guide book.

Above right In the continuing belt of trees and gardens alongside Tower Promenade was the **FAIRY GLEN MINIATURE RAILWAY, NEW BRIGHTON**, an 18-inch-gauge steam railway that was one of the children's fairground rides in the Tower Amusement Park from 1948 to 1965. This locomotive and its three coaches came second-hand from the Jaywick Miniature Railway near Clacton. The enclosed bogie coaches were built in 1936, each with two spacious compartments furnished with comfortable, foam-rubber seats in moquette and mahogany seat and window frames, and were electrically lit by coach-mounted, dynamo-charged batteries. The 0-4-0 locomotive, No 5854 *Tim Bobbin*, was built in 1939 with a vertical boiler in the cab, an oil-burning Stanley steam car engine and chain drive to the two axles. The engine and coaches were painted in Southern Railway green with cream roofs. Restricted by the narrow confines of the site, the ride was for 200 yards from a double-track stub terminus along a single-track route through floral gardens with a tight 40-foot-radius loop past the rock face of a disused quarry and through an artificial tunnel rather like Santa Claus's grotto, with a waterwheel at its entrance and an illuminated model fairground on a ledge inside.

The railway was the main feature of Uncle Tommy's Kiddies' Playground, wedged in a narrow strip along the promenade side of the sloping fairground. The concessionaire, Tommy Mann, also operated the Marine Lake between the fort causeway and the bathing pool on the other side of the pier. In 1951 he added a conventional coal-burning 4-4-2 locomotive, *Crompton*, an open carriage, an overall-roof station and a two-road engine shed on a spur off the loop. The locomotives bore the legend 'TME' (Tommy Mann's Enterprises). Charlie Mann took over the children's fairground in the mid-1950s and rebodied *Crompton* with LMS crimson 'Coronation' Class streamlining. *Tim Bobbin*, shown here, retired in 1959 to be replaced by a second-hand 1945 Ruston & Hornsby diesel. The saloon coaches of 1936 were in service till the railway closed in 1965, when all the rolling-stock went to other miniature railways and collections.

The turret of the northernmost house on the riverside promenade peers through the trees. *Harvey Barton postcard*

Right It is early morning on the **TOWER PROMENADE, NEW BRIGHTON**. The lone figure in the middle of the road emphasises the deserted promenade, which, with the shuttered shops, theatre and fairground and the sunny morning haze over the river, looks like a hibernating resort on the open sea, but this was a morning in August 1954 and we are looking up the River Mersey. Later in the day the haze would clear to unveil the port of Liverpool on the left horizon and the scene would be animated with crowds of holidaymakers and day-trippers from the north Midlands who came to New Brighton in the summer. The bollards across the road mark the beginning of the 2¼-mile

walk along the traffic-free riverside promenade to Seacombe Ferry. The wooden trestle structure of the scenic railway stands among the trees, cars on the gravity run skimming over the treetops and down through the foliage on what the cartoonist Rowland Emett would have called a true branch line. This was part of the Tower Amusement Park on the slopes below New Brighton Tower (1900), a massive, ornate building in glazed red brick housing a theatre and ballroom, once the base of a lattice steel tower like Blackpool's but taller. On the corner of Egerton Street (right) stands the Tivoli Theatre, which opened in 1914 as a vaudeville theatre. After the Second World War the 636-seat theatre staged variety shows in summer and repertory plays in winter. It closed in 1955. S. Reece's Tivoli Café occupied the entire first-floor frontage of the theatre, and under the cast-iron and glass canopy were a gift shop and five empty shops at the time of this photograph.

Above Bank holiday at New Brighton: this view from the Tower Building shows the Cheshire seaside resort at the peak of its prosperity in the post-war period, with crowds of holidaymakers and day-trippers on the sands, the fairground, the pier and the ferry. On the slope below the Tower Building was the **TOWER AMUSEMENT PARK**, which included the scenic railway and the big wheel that we see in the foreground, together with a motor-racing circuit, zoo, helter-skelter, motor boating pool, Noah's Ark, ghost train, bumper cars, 'whip', 'caterpillar', sideshows and a children's fairground including the

Fairy Glen Miniature Railway. The Tower Grounds extended behind the Tower Building to include an athletics stadium, which was the home of New Brighton Football & Athletic Club from 1946 to 1976. *Commercial postcard*

Below What was called **NEW BRIGHTON PIER**, and appeared from every other angle to be a single pier, can be seen from this angle to have been two piers: the functional Ferry Pier (right) and the Promenade Pier or pleasure pier (left) alongside. The first Ferry Pier (1833-67) was a humble, timber structure

with sheds on deck. The new pier of 1867, 600 feet long on iron piles screwed into the bedrock, with a bridge to a floating stage, was engineered by James Brunlees to the same design as his New Ferry Pier of 1865. Brunlees is better known for his piers at Southport and Southend, and the Mersey Railway tunnel. The tollhouse, halfway along the pier, was enlarged in 1928 in Art Deco style. The word 'STEAMERS' was displayed in lights on a gantry across the pier entrance.

The Promenade Pier was one of 14 engineered by Eugenius Birch (1814-84), famous for his structures at Margate, Blackpool North and Brighton West. He built New Brighton Pier in 1866-67, again on screw piles. This pier was 550 feet long and the deck ranged up to 130 feet in width, standing higher than the Ferry Pier and the promenade. New Brighton Pier Company closed the pier in 1923 because it was unsafe, and the local council, which owned the Ferry Pier from 1861, did not buy it till 1928. Over the next two years it was rebuilt with a steel substructure and reinforcement, and a new, silver-domed circular pavilion and café, and re-opened in 1930. This 1950s picture postcard shows the two piers on a typical cold, grey day on the Mersey riviera, with everyone dressed in suits and overcoats and Bootle docks on the horizon – not quite the seaside holiday picture New Brighton publicists painted. Pier entertainments were a holiday song-and-dance show, dancing twice daily, marionettes and Sunday band concerts. The ferry closed in 1971 and the Ferry Pier was dismantled in 1973. The Promenade Pier closed in 1972 and disappeared in 1978. *Tuck's postcard*

This page **NEW BRIGHTON SANDS** were the resort's focal point at the junction of the promenade, pier and main street. On a sunny August morning in 1952 the beach slowly comes to life as well-dressed mothers and children settle down in deckchairs in the lee of the rock-faced sandstone wall of Tower Promenade, and in the foreground a girl in a black overcoat makes a sandcastle watched by a black dog. Caravans selling shellfish and mineral waters are still shuttered at the foot of the wide slipway from the promenade. The entrance of the Ferry Pier is on the right, spanned by a gantry with the word 'STEAMERS', illuminated by night. Coloured lights are strung from the lamp posts along and across the promenade. Opposite the pier the cream stuccoed Royal Ferry Hotel (left) and the red-brick Avondale Café, with its cupola, flank the entrance of the main street, Victoria Road. The original part of the hotel stands on the corner of Victoria Road with a parapet and rusticated ground-floor elevation and cornerstones in cream stucco in early-Victorian Italianate style. The two-bay elevation we see from the sands was the side of the hotel – the front faced Victoria Road. It was built about 1850 as the Ferry Hotel, renamed the Royal Hotel in 1867 and the Royal Ferry Hotel in 1869. A ten-bay extension along Tower Promenade was built in 1926 in Italianate style with wide eaves, iron balconies and two entrances from the promenade in the rusticated ground-floor elevation continued from the original hotel. Paddy's mobile oyster bar was a branch of a business in Grange Road, Birkenhead – he also had a stall on the Tower Amusement Park.

Above The rock-faced red-sandstone **NEW BRIGHTON PROMENADE** wall, which extends all the way from Seacombe Ferry, continues past New Brighton Pier around the bend of Marine Promenade, built in 1906-08, on Rock Point from the Mersey to the Irish Sea. The water, gleaming in the backlight of diffused morning sunshine, laps the wall and slipway. From an abutment in the wall, a ramp leads up to the deck of the Promenade Pier with its shelters, while the word 'STEAMERS' is silhouetted at the entrance of the Ferry Pier alongside. The columns of both piers stand clear of the water level in this half-tide scene, showing them jutting out into the Mersey on a sandbank or bar where the river meets the sea, and we can see the tops of the concrete piles inserted at the base of the columns when Wallasey Corporation rebuilt the Promenade Pier in

1928-30. The street lamps have been 'streamlined' in this 1960 view, and the Avondale Café and Royal Ferry Hotel stand on the right at the entrance of Victoria Road.

Below Happy days on **NEW BRIGHTON SANDS**: the receding tide has left a crowd in deckchairs by the sea wall against a backdrop of the Promenade Pier with its windbreaks and pavilions and the ferry steamer *J. Farley* alongside the landing stage. The Ferry Pier is marked by the hipped roof of the tollhouse halfway along. *From British Railways Holiday Guide, 1950*

Above right A low-tide scene on another grey day at **NEW BRIGHTON**: this was the view north of the pier down the Mersey estuary to the open sea and the sand dunes along the Lancashire coast stretching to Formby Point. Everybody on the beach is fully dressed, but the deckchairs and beach stalls are out and the children are digging in the sand. The view is from the Victoria Road frontage of the Royal Ferry Hotel, and across the street are the distinctive turret and cupola on the corner of the Avondale Café, with tables for the hardy on the balcony on the roof of the colonnade spanning the footpath. Marine Promenade was built in 1906-08 and gives access to the causeway leading across the rocks to Perch Rock Fort, which is surrounded by the sea at

high tide. A trench has been cut through the rock to lay a sewer running out to sea. *Tuck's postcard*

Below As ferry passengers walked off the pier 100 years ago, this was what they saw: the wide bellmouth of Victoria Road main street sloping up between the Royal Ferry Hotel (left) and the Avondale Café (right). The place was clean and tidy and the people were well-dressed. This spacious street scene was the setting for the New Brighton tram terminus; the photograph must have been taken after 1907, when the four tram sidings shown here replaced the horseshoe loop by the pier entrance and the cars arrived along Virginia Road and left by Victoria Road instead of the other way round as before. A car is seen emerging from Virginia Road to drop into one of the double-track sidings by the Royal Ferry Hotel. Two cars occupy the double-track siding on the right alongside a large passenger shelter next to Francis Storey's Bon Marché fancy goods shop below the Avondale Café. This shop was established by Alderman Francis Storey (b1845), an Irish immigrant who became Mayor of Wallasey in 1912-13 and chairman of the Ferries Committee; the Wallasey ferry steamer *Francis Storey* (1922-51) was named after him, posthumously. His gift shop is seen here before the erection of the glazed iron colonnade around it that most of us remember. As a creation of the Victorian and Edwardian period, New Brighton was still a new town when this photograph was taken, so it is no surprise to find that this scene hardly changed at all over the next 50 years, as we shall see in the next two photographs. *Photochrom postcard*

Below The **AVONDALE CAFÉ, NEW BRIGHTON**, was a handsome key landmark of the townscape and waterfront. It was built in 1904 in glazed red brick trimmed with yellow terracotta, sporting a cupola on the corner turret and a wide cast-iron and glass colonnade spanning the full width of the footpath and spreading the full length of the frontage around the corner from Marine Promenade (right) into Victoria Road,

with four bays each side of the corner portico. Almost 50 years after the previous Edwardian view, the Café still occupied the first and second floors while the ground floor under the colonnade still housed Storey's Bon Marché fancy goods shop, selling gifts, toys, cakes, tobacco, cigarettes, etc. An adjoining colonnade extends from the Bon Marché up the slope of Victoria Road around the corner into Virginia Road. This

colonnade fronted a single-storey building housing a public shelter and lavatories, formerly the Corporation Tramways waiting room and 'cloak rooms', as this wide street scene was the site of the former New Brighton tram terminus until closure in 1933. The shelter occupied the three window bays next to the Bon Marché. The lavatories, on the corner of Virginia Road, were a beautifully anachronistic showpiece of ornate Edwardian ceramics with polished brass and copper fittings. They were fit for the Victoria & Albert Museum and were always apparently maintained with some pride. This is another cold, grey, windy day in 1952 at New Brighton, as cloth-capped men in tweed jackets and long overcoats walk across the wide, empty street, and there

were so few motor vehicles about that there was no need for road markings, a pedestrian crossing or a refuge island.

Left **VICTORIA ROAD, NEW BRIGHTON**, sloped up from the pier past the shops and the steeple of St James's Church to the villas on the hill. In 1954 a 1948 Wallasey bus, tall and narrow, looking sunny in primrose and cream, and smartly trimmed with string courses of black beading, has turned out of Virginia Road bus station (right) to climb the slope of Victoria Road at the start of its 5¼-mile journey on route 17 to Wallasey, Poulton and Seacombe. On the right is the corner of the ornate, glazed, iron colonnade around the public lavatories of the former tram terminus, now serving the bus station. Behind the trees are the Douglas Tea Rooms & Dining Rooms (selling dinners from 1s 6d to 2s 3d), William Brice's café, Samuel Warrington's restaurant, Maxim's café, Alice Wynbeck's milk bar and fried fish shop, Paddy's seafood bar and J. & F. Morris's café. Beyond the trees on the right we can just see the canopy of the Trocadero Cinema, while on the left, bracketed to a lamp post, a signboard with a black hand points across the street 'to bus loading station'. Beyond is a succession of restaurants, cafés, toy shops, a pin-table saloon and The New Empress Ballroom, and a bakery van is unloading cakes at one of the restaurants. A solitary street lamp is suspended from a cable slung across the street between two former tramway traction poles. St James's Church in the background was designed by George Gilbert Scott and built in 1854-56 for the residents of the villas of early New Brighton up the hill. Not much has changed here since the time of our earlier Edwardian view. The trees have grown, the

colonnade has been erected, some of the street furniture and shops have changed, and fashions have changed – but people are still well dressed, in overcoats, hats and school uniform. The motor bus has replaced the electric tramcar but it still arrives by Virginia Road, leaves by Victoria Road and follows a former tram route to Seacombe.

Above We are now looking down **VICTORIA ROAD, NEW BRIGHTON**, the town's main shopping street, towards the pier in 1954. The Post Office stands on the corner of Waterloo Road (left), and next to it is the canopy of the Court Cinema, New Brighton's first purpose-built cinema, opened in 1912; it closed in 1958. The Trocadero Cinema was further down on the left-hand side of the street. Grosvenor Street is on the right with Len Harrison's grocery shop on the corner. Most of the shops for the residents, such as butchers, fishmongers and greengrocers, were at this upper end of the main street, while most of the cafés, fish and chip shops, gift shops and pin-table saloons for the visitors were at the lower end towards the pier. The 1874 Ordnance Survey map shows the south (right) side of Victoria Road completely built up to the Victoria Hotel but nothing on the north side except for the isolated Napoleon Buildings housing the Post Office. The left-hand side of the street was not complete till about 1900. The sparsely spaced street lamps hang from the long arms of former tramway traction poles (stripped of their ornamentation), which used to suspend the overhead electric wire above the single line along the middle of the street until the last electric cars passed through here in 1933.

Above Peace on the prom: the tide is low in the Mersey estuary and the lonely cry of a seabird or the mournful boom of a distant foghorn is all that breaks the silence of this bleak morning scene in 1954 on **MARINE PROMENADE, NEW BRIGHTON**, with its elegant Edwardian iron shelters and wooden seats. Two lone promenaders sit and watch the dim silhouette of a steam coaster making its way out to sea through the mist that veils the backdrop of Liverpool's northern dockland just over a mile away.

Below **ROUGH SEA AT NEW BRIGHTON**: driven by a north-easterly gale out of an angry sky, a wild Irish Sea crashes over the offshore fort and sea wall at Rock Point, viewed here from the Promenade Pier. The Emetty pagoda-style pavilions on the promenade offer little shelter from the spray, but there are few promenaders out today to see this winter spectacle. The

storm transforms the character of the resort so familiar to summer holidaymakers, and the golden sands of bucket and spade days are 12 feet under high water. *1938 Valentine's postcard*

Above right The bend in the promenade west of the pier takes us round the corner of the Wirral peninsula from the River Mersey to the Irish Sea and now we are on the seaward side of Wallasey, which faces north across Liverpool Bay and along the dunes of the Lancashire coast to Formby Point. This section of **MARINE PROMENADE, NEW BRIGHTON**, was built between 1906 and 1908, but the buildings on the right are older and used to front on to the beach. Union Terrace, of two-storey houses, was built about 1840 and some of those terraced houses still survive among the big hotels on the seafront between the foot of Waterloo Road and the foot of Rowson Street; the hotels seen here replaced some of the terraced houses. From the right

we see the Café Royal, the Grand Hotel and the Queen's Royal Hotel. The Grand Hotel, with balconies on the first and second floors and a parapet, was formerly the Marine Hotel, built circa 1845, enlarged in about 1915 and renamed the Grand Hotel in 1930. Before the promenade was built, the expanse of the sandy beach reached right up to the front garden walls of the buildings on Union Terrace, but has been replaced by an expanse of tarmac. The two post-war vans parked in front of the terrace in 1954 are an Austin K8 Three Way and a utility-looking Morris Commercial.

Below Seen across the dammed waters of the 10-acre Marine Lake, the red sandstone **PERCH ROCK FORT AND LIGHTHOUSE, NEW BRIGHTON**, is reached at low water by a causeway from Marine Promenade. It was an artillery garrison from 1829 till 1954 to guard the entrance of the port of Liverpool. The lighthouse beyond the fort, in this half-tide 1963 scene, is also accessible at low water. It was built in 1827-30 to replace the first navigation light erected there in 1683 on a perch, a wooden post supported by a tripod, marking low rocks by Rock Channel. The lighthouse is 90 feet tall and built of dovetailed blocks of Anglesey granite, mortared and sheathed with volcanic ash that set harder than the granite. The light had a range of 14 miles but was shut down in 1973 as Rock

Channel was silted and disused. A motor coaster butts up Crosby Channel in the background.

When the fort was built in 1826-29, bristling with guns, it stood off a wild headland, its garrison waiting for an armada that never came. Instead, holidaymakers surrounded the fort as the town of New Brighton appeared at the other end of the causeway. The guns were fired on only three occasions: at the start of the two World Wars in 1914 and 1939, both as vain stop signals to incoming sailing vessels whose crews did not realise war had been declared, and once in anger during the Second War at what was thought to be a U-boat in Liverpool Bay. In 1914 the first shot was too high and the shell landed in the dunes at Hightown on the other side of the estuary; the gun was lowered and the second shot hit the bows of a liner at anchor. An indignant resident took the first shell in a bucket to Seaforth battery, where it was put on display with the placard: 'A present from New Brighton'. The 1939 incident was with a fishing smack in Rock Channel, which had been closed for the war. During the Second World War the concrete radar tower (left) and searchlight dome (right) were added and the fort was camouflaged as a tea garden; the roof was painted green with the word 'TEAS' in white. The fort was decommissioned in 1954, sold in 1958 and opened to the public as part of the New Brighton holiday scene.

Above Out in the wide open spaces of King's Parade, boys are masters of their own vessels in the Lilliput world of the **MODEL YACHT POND, NEW BRIGHTON,** and spend hours fascinated by watching the sleek hulls of their sailing craft – many of them Star Yachts of Birkenhead – scudding across this purpose-built pond when the sails are set right for the wind. The expansive 1930s promenade is a pleasant place to be on a fine sunny day, with the backdrop of marine villas of early New Brighton rising prominently on the hillside – but this promenade was a massive land reclamation that buried acres of fine, clean sandy shore and the sandstone cliffs, promontories and caves that were New Brighton's sole natural asset. Only the tops of the Yellow Noses and Red Noses survive above ground.

King's Parade was an extension of Marine Promenade from

New Brighton to Wallasey beach, and the first stretch, from the foot of Waterloo Road to the Red Noses, was built in 1931-34. This was part of an ambitious scheme that also created the Marine Lake, the famous New Brighton Bathing Pool (left), a sunken car park and the model yacht pond. When the bathing pool opened in 1934 this modern Art Deco stadium was said to be the largest swimming pool in the world, designed to hold 4,000 bathers and 20,000 spectators. The pool was 330 feet by 225 feet and the depth ranged from an extensive shallow area for toddlers on the north side to 15 feet for divers on the south side. This was the scene of the Miss New Brighton bathing beauty contest from 1949 to 1989. In 1990 heavy seas undermined the foundations of the pool and another landmark disappeared from the New Brighton seafront. *1936 Valentine's postcard*

Below left The **RED NOSES AND TOWER, NEW BRIGHTON**, the resort's two greatest attractions, are seen in one Edwardian picture postcard, a record of lost amenities. This sandy beach and the low sandstone cliffs, bluffs and caves west of Atherton Street were embedded in the King's Parade in 1931-39. In the background rises New Brighton Tower, 621 feet high, built in 1897-1900 and demolished in 1919-21 for lack of maintenance during the First World War. *Commercial postcard*

Top right The marine villas of early New Brighton were built along Wellington Road and Montpellier Crescent with views over Liverpool Bay. The houses on **WELLINGTON ROAD, NEW BRIGHTON**, like No 42 'Portland Villa' seen here in 1978, were built on the steep slope traversed by the gradients of the intersecting Atherton Street and Portland Street, running down to the north shore. Thus what appear to be single-storey houses, or bungalows, at the front on Wellington Road are two-storey houses at the back as they face out over their long, sloping back gardens and King's Parade; likewise, the two-storey houses are three storeys facing the sea. It is disputable which are the fronts and backs of these villas as both sides have similar architectural treatment; the seaward elevations, being taller, are more impressive, but the modest, human-scale front elevations of the one/two-storey villas viewed from Wellington Road have more charm. 'Portland Villa' was built in 1834 for Adam Dugdale, a Liverpool cornbroker. This was a period when it was the vogue to build single-storey 'marine residences' at nascent 'fashionable watering places' like New Brighton and Southport faced in stucco with late-Regency classical features combined with features of the early Gothic revival. He we see Regency pilasters, frieze and a low-pitched roof combined with Gothic windows with strong vertical lines of thick glazing bars and narrow, arched panes, framed by rectangular hood mouldings, or dripstones. Regency architecture was the last phase of the Georgian period and antiquarians introduced Gothic details into Georgian towards the end of the 18th century to add a certain picturesque quaintness, and called it Gothick with a 'k'.

Above Standing on the corner of Wellington Road and the steep slope of Portland Street is No 46, another modest single-storey house with two storeys at the back and an elevated view of the sea over the long, sloping back garden. It has a low-pitched roof with wide Italianate eaves, and the symmetrical three-bay front is divided by split pilasters with Gothick arches. The house was built in 1835 for Reginald Hargreaves, a Burnley cotton spinner. It was originally 'Horton Villa' but was renamed 'Villa Marina' circa 1900, and became the Blue Horizon Café in 1937 – the blue horizon can be seen in the background. In 1957 the house was divided into two maisonettes.

Above A feature of the townscape were the steep streets sloping down the side of the Wallasey plateau to the Mersey at Egremont and Upper Brighton and down to the Irish Sea at New Brighton. **ATHERTON STREET, NEW BRIGHTON,** runs from the highest part of the town, 190 feet, down to the promenade in 600 yards, with maximum gradients of 1 in 8, levelling out as it crosses Albion Street, Victoria Road and Wellington Road, passing the fronts of New Brighton station and the adjacent Winter Gardens Cinema on the way. The expanse of King's Parade lays across the foot of the hill and the Irish Sea is spread out before us in this 1954 view. Atherton Street is named after the founder of New Brighton, James Atherton, a retired Liverpool merchant, who first developed villas on the heights of Everton, then a rustic village, between 1800 and 1830. The growth of Liverpool made him turn his attention to the Cheshire bank, and in 1830 he bought (what is variously recorded as) 127, 170 or 180 acres of heath and dunes at Perch Rock Point, Liscard. From 1832 he sold plots on a street

plan and prospectus for a 'fashionable watering place'. Both his Everton and New Brighton developments were to enable professional Liverpool gentlemen to escape the industry and squalor of the city. Rock Ferry was a similar development by the Royal Rock Ferry Company in 1836.

Below left Edward Riley's bow-fronted chemist's shop in a neat classical building rounded off the fork junction of **ALBION STREET, NEW BRIGHTON** (left) and Montpellier Crescent (right). This is the top end of Albion Street on the bosky heights of New Brighton in 1954, with the early-Victorian marine villas of Montpellier Crescent behind the trees on the right. Riley's was No 60 Albion Street and there was a parade of seven shops beyond on the right-hand side. There are elegant Edwardian bench seats among the bushes on the small roundabout with its gas lamp at this five-way junction, and there is little motor traffic to cause a nuisance to anyone taking a rest here. Portland Street is to the right, running steeply down to the sea, and Dudley Road to the left, climbing higher into the residential area. Buses on route 5 from Seacombe Ferry emerged from Dudley Road and turned round here from 1929 to 1944, when the route was extended down Albion Street and Atherton Street to New Brighton station. This was route 15 from 1951.

Above right Some of the early villas were built of local red sandstone. One of them was 'Warrenside' at 31-33 **MONTPELLIER CRESCENT, NEW BRIGHTON**, opposite Mount Road. It was built in 1841-42 as one house of classical proportions with an Italian Ionic colonnaded portico, a small pediment above a recessed window flanked by coupled pilasters, and a parapet hiding a low-pitched roof. The back of the house had a central bow projection facing out over the sea. The house was later divided into two, with an extension on the left-hand side in matching ashlar sandstone with a classical porch and a panelled front door. 'Warrenside' was first the home of Mr W. H. Gilliatt, a merchant, and finally, from 1939, of the Scott family of bakers before succumbing to decay and demolition. It was photographed in 1978.

Below The grimy sandstone wall on the right is founded on an outcrop of sandstone bedrock on the summit of **MOUNT ROAD, NEW BRIGHTON**, at its junction with Stoneby Drive (left), looking north to the steeple of New Brighton Presbyterian Church in 1963. The Edwardian houses are faced with Ruabon pressed red brick with stone window sills and lintels. Mount Road was on the old road from Seacombe Ferry to New Brighton before Seabank Road was built. It terminates in Montpellier Crescent, the fashionable part of the early residential 'watering place'.

Above left Solid homes built in the first 30 years of the 20th century up and down quiet roads lined with trees and gas lamps, like **MOUNT ROAD, NEW BRIGHTON**, seen here, evoke the character of this part of the town between St George's Mount and Rockland Road, the highest part of New Brighton and Wallasey. This 1954 picture was taken from the corner of Gorsehill Road with its covered reservoirs and water tower supplying the island townships with water from Birkenhead's Alwen Dam in Denbighshire and from local boreholes. Sandymount Road is on the left with views along the Wirral coast to the mountains of north Wales.

Left Poised dramatically in the fork between North Drive (left) and Ennerdale Road (right), on the steep slope down to Warren Drive, **NEW BRIGHTON PRESBYTERIAN CHURCH** was built in 1909-10 in the Ruabon pressed red brick and neo-Gothic ecclesiastical style of the period. It was funded by Frederick North (1832-1910), a solicitor, of Wellington Road, who owned the land on which North Drive and the church were built. This handsome, lofty building, photographed in 1954, formed a fitting cornerpiece at this dipped road junction, maintaining the elevation of the houses above it and towering majestically above Warren Drive as it passed the broad gap of Ennerdale Drive below the church. Its steeple was a landmark on the New Brighton skyline.

Above Window on Wallasey: this is the south end of **MARLOWE ROAD, WALLASEY**, in 1950, with Thorncliffe Road to the right and Mill Lane crossing at the signals at the end of the road. Woodstock Road continues south towards Birkenhead. The 1950s came in with new concrete architecture and street furniture although there was little money at this time for new buildings except in blitzed city centres like Coventry and Plymouth and for the 1951 Festival of Britain in London. 1950s-style concrete lamp posts with electric lights were beginning to replace iron gas lamps along the road from Birkenhead to New Brighton, and by night they shone with a turquoise glow, which cast a fairyland touch over the street scene. The concrete shelter at the bus stop has a corrugated asbestos roof. Buses on five services stopped there, and from this window we could watch a frequent succession of primrose Wallasey buses and blue Birkenhead buses on routes 9 to Charing Cross, 10 to Woodside and New Ferry, 11 to Higher Tranmere, 17 to Seacombe and 18 to Upton and Woodchurch. Bread was delivered to your home by the humming battery-powered Morrison Electricar of 1949 (left). This photograph had to be taken in winter, as summer foliage completely masked all the houses seen here.

Above The township of Wallasey begins here in **MARLOWE ROAD, WALLASEY** – this is the southern entrance on the road from Birkenhead after passing through Poulton. Wallasey town lies on the west side of the island of the same name, north of Poulton and west of Liscard and New Brighton. This 1954 view is from Mill Lane crossing to Marlowe Road Congregational Church at the junction with Torrington Road. Marlowe Road was built in 1909 under the Wallasey Tramways & Improvements Act to pave the way for the electric tramway extension from Poulton to Wallasey village and on to New Brighton. The first three pairs of semi-detached houses on each side of the road were built in 1909 as a physical extension of the built-up area of Poulton, with fields separating them from the houses in Liscard and the rest of Wallasey. Residential development followed in the wake of the opening of the line in 1911. Marlowe Road chapel opened in 1913 and by that time the houses extended into Torrington Road and Cliff Road. Wallasey grew out of a village into a town and the rural area between it and Liscard was filled in with houses in the 1920s

and '30s. The 1948 Wallasey bus, stopping at the shelter we saw in the last picture, is Seacombe-bound on route 17, which succeeded the P tram line when Wallasey tramways closed in 1933.

Below This is the wide three-way junction of Marlowe Road (centre and right), Torrington Road (left) and Cliff Road (extreme right), looking south from Marlowe Road Congregational Church towards Woodstock Road. The signs on the railing at the apex beyond the flower bed point to New Brighton (left) and Wallasey Beach (right) in larger capitals than those on the black and white signpost above it. Few people, even in these large houses, owned cars. A resident with a leather shopping bag waits for a bus, and the streets look tidy with no parked vehicles. Indeed, there are only two moving cars in this picture, together with two cyclists and one parked bicycle in this placid afternoon scene in 1952. The nearer one of the two approaching cars is an early 1930s Austin taxicab, which broke down as it passed the bus stop.

Cast-iron and glass colonnades spanned with full width of the footpath by the parades of shops on **WALLASEY ROAD, WALLASEY,** from the corner of Belvidere Road (right) to the corner of Newland Drive. The colonnades provided shade from the sun and shelter from the rain for window-shoppers and they were well preserved, featuring convex glazing and the shop names or merchandise displayed in white lettering in a coloured glass fascia. On the first block in 1963 are N. Burrows (fried fish), William Brown (hardware and ironmongery), W. N. Parkinson (coal office), Miss Mabel Smethurst (costumier), Mrs Florence England (fancy draper), F. Vaughan (newsagent), Hawkings & Hunter

(electrical contractors), Mrs Mary Keen (florist) and Charles Plant (greengrocer). There was a break at Westwood Grove, a small cul-de-sac, then the colonnaded shops continued to the corner of Newland Drive on the brow of Wallasey Road with C. Hartley (grocer), Whitby's Dairies, Birkenhead & District Co-operative Society (grocery), Arthur Williams (upholsterer), Smith's (chandler), F. Wilkinson (glass and paint), Johnson's (cleaners and dyers) and United Co-op Laundries. This was the road to Wallasey from Liscard and the shops are an extension of Liscard's shops over the township boundary by the Boot Inn into Wallasey.

Above This is the northern half of **SEAVIEW ROAD, WALLASEY**; the southern part, beyond Massey Park, is in Liscard. We are looking north in 1963 from the corner of Turret Road (right), with Kingsway on the left. The sea view is now blocked by the houses on the left and the shops on the bend into Mount Pleasant Road. This is a characteristic Wallasey scene: the wide, quiet, tree-shaded road, wide flagstoned footpaths, Ruabon brick walls, sandstone gateposts and solid Edwardian houses with walls of Ruabon brick and grey roughcast with polygonal corner towers and spirelets.

Below Crossing the road was no worry for Wallaseyans in the 1950s, and in those days of full employment for men, when women kept house, the streets were peopled mainly by women

out shopping or on their way to a cookery demonstration at the Art Deco electricity showrooms. In 1954 two smartly dressed women with leather shopping bags cross **BELVIDERE ROAD, WALLASEY**, and two women in frocks – one holding a bicycle with a shopping basket on the front – leisurely converse by the sunshade outside the chemist's shop on the left. We are looking north from Broadway Avenue (right and left), and the shops on the left, from the corner, are Charles Leggett (chemist, photo and ciné dealer), Harry Amis & Sons (fruiterer), John Atkinson (grocer) and N. & I. Wilson (newsagents). Belvidere Road continues north into Rolleston Drive, where a Wallasey bus on route 6 recedes into the distance towards Grove Road.

Above True to its name, **BROADWAY AVENUE, WALLASEY,** is broad and lined with trees, with bushes along the grass verge on the right. It lies east-west, linking the two north-south arteries, Belvidere Road and Claremount Road, and runs from the back of the bus garage off Seaview Road to St Hilary's Church, which we see rising above the trees, on the ridge of Claremount Road. The granite setts paving the entrance to Belvidere Recreation Ground, the elegant wooden Edwardian bench seat and the Ruabon brick walls and sandstone gateposts beyond the corner of Shrewsbury Road (left) are characteristic features of the Wallasey townscape. Parked on the right of this 1954 view is a 1951 Austin A40 van.

Below **CLAREMOUNT ROAD, WALLASEY,** runs along the western ridge of the Wallasey plateau with side streets dropping away on both sides, but more steeply on the west. We are looking south in 1954 at the crossing of Broadway Avenue (left) and Broadway (right), shelving steeply to Wallasey Village, the former village street. St Hilary's Church dominates the scene on the corner of Broadway. Such was the camber that buses on route 17 along Claremount Road in both directions leaned over to the west as they passed Broadway and Mayfield Road. Broadway was formerly Folly Lane, a footpath down the north side of the churchyard, rebuilt in 1910-11 as Broadway for trams on line P, which were fitted with mechanical track brakes for the 1 in 11 gradient. At the top of the slope is a British Railways parcels and luggage van, a Karrier of about 1940, while parked on the left is a 1948 Standard Vanguard car.

Above **ST HILARY'S CHURCH, WALLASEY**, the majestic, black, parish church that crowns the Wallasey ridge, was built in 1858-59 on a Celtic foundation dating back to the 5th century. It was built of local sandstone from the quarry (later the bowling green) opposite the Little Brighton Inn in Upper Brighton. The church is designed on the plan of a cross with the nave and transepts radiating north, south, east and west from a central tower, all in the Victorian Decorated/Perpendicular Gothic ecclesiastical architecture of its period. The sandstone of the fabric and the graves in the churchyard have weathered grimy black on the height above Merseyside during 100 years of the Coal Age, but this makes the church stand out bold and impressive like the Liver Building on Liverpool waterfront. Most of the painted and stained-glass

windows were damaged in the air raids in 1940-41 and a new east window was installed in 1955, overlooking Claremont Road, from which this photograph was taken in 1951.

The present church is the sixth on the site, earlier churches having been rebuilt after fire damage. There has been a rector of Wallasey since circa 1170, when the first stone church was built. In subsequent rebuildings, the Norman font was put out in the rectory garden and in 1900 it went into the new church of St Luke's, Poulton. The first church was built on this site in about 446. It was founded by Bishop (later Saint) Germanus of Auxerre in central Gaul, a missionary to the Britons in the 5th century, shortly before the Teutonic invasions. Wallasey Church is one of only eight churches in Britain dedicated to St Hilary, five being in Wales, one in Cornwall and one in Lincolnshire. St Hilary was not a woman but a man – a 4th-century Bishop of Poitiers in western Gaul, whose Roman orthodox Christian teachings Germanus preached in Britain to suppress Celtic Christian 'heresy', a disbelief in original sin, baptism and predestination. St Hilary's Day is 13 January, and his name is given to the Hilary Law Sittings, a session of the High Court, and to the Hilary term at Oxford and Dublin universities.

Below left Looking up **CHURCH HILL, WALLASEY**, in 1961 we see the old rectory, the clock tower of St Hilary's Church and the ruin of the previous church tower on the west slope of the Wallasey ridge above the south end of the former village street. Sunlight gleams on the south dial of the chiming clock installed in the church tower in 1895 in memory of William Chambres of Wallasey Grange (now a public park). The ruined tower dates from the 13th century in its lower part, while the upper part has the datestone 1530. The church of 1530 was rebuilt in 1760, but was ruined in 1857 by a fire caused by the grocer-sexton smoking his bacon in the boilerhouse and

zealously stoking up the boilers because of complaints about the cold church – the melting fat started the fire. The stone rectory was built in 1632 and extended in 1695 in brick and again in 1864 with stone from the ruins of Wallasey Hall (former home of the Meols family), which stood between the church and the rectory. A new rectory was built in 1940 on the site of Wallasey Hall and the old rectory was used for church meetings for the next 36 years. It is now restored as a private house.

Below The main street of Wallasey is called **WALLASEY VILLAGE**, a name that, like Liscard Village, defines the extent of the former one-street village. The village street straggled half a mile from the foot of Church Hill to the corner of Green Lane, though today the street name Wallasey Village extends to the corner of Grove Road. The old village street was very narrow – only 6 feet across at the old Cheshire Cheese Inn – and has been successively widened since 1885 and lined with new buildings, completely losing any semblance of village character. This 1952 postcard shows just another period in the widening and urbanisation of Wallasey Village, a process that has continued. It shows the parade of shops from the corner of Perrin Road (right): Mrs Lucy Gilbert (confectioner), William McMinn (chandler), William Moody & Sons (boot and shoe dealers), Henry Godfrey (outfitter) and D. Williams & Son (grocers). Beyond that, in a recess of road widening, we can see the timber framework of the Black Horse Hotel. The shops on the left, of D. Tate (greengrocer), Gerard Booth (newsagent) and Heaps & Jones (building contractors), take us to the corner of Stonehouse Road. From this viewpoint outside the Parish Hall we can see the main part of the former village street to where it narrowed beyond the corner of Leasowe Road. The 1946 Wallasey bus is on route 2 from Harrison Drive to Seacombe Ferry via Liscard and Egremont. *Valentine's postcard*

Above The junction of **WALLASEY VILLAGE** and Leasowe Road was the centre of the former village, with a lamp post and trough where the pedestrian island is seen here in 1955. Leasowe Road succeeded Green Lane as the only road to the former Wallasey island, along the alluvial coast, and in the 1950s there were only three other roads into Wallasey, all over dock bridges across the former Wallasey Pool. The shops on the left are Strong's Dairy milk bar, Ainsworth's confectionery shop, Wallasey Post Office, Eunice Kevan (fancy draper) and A. Cheetham (ladies' hairdresser). A garden wall follows the line of the shop fronts, and behind the front gardens are houses fronting on to the main street. In line with the houses is the Black Horse Hotel, with applied Tudor-style timber framework;

it was built in 1931 when the old Black Horse of 1722 was demolished to widen the road. The hotel's name is believed to commemorate one of England's earliest racecourses, a 5-mile circuit between the north end of Wallasey village and Leasowe Castle in the 17th and 18th centuries. On the right-hand side of the street, from the corner of Leasowe Road, we see E. B. Jones ('Quality' baker), Birkenhead & District Co-operative Society (grocery), and, beyond Lycett Street, Celia Manley (chemist). A 1954 Morris Minor car has just passed the street junction, two Wallasey buses stand at shelters outside the Black Horse bound for Seacombe, and behind the buses we see the projecting block with the parade of shops we saw in the previous picture. *Valentine's postcard*

Left **OLD WALLASEY VILLAGE** was the last remnant of the narrow village street between Leasowe Road and Sandy Lane, demolished in 1950. This circa 1938 view is looking north through the double bend from the corner of Beechwood Drive (left). The Corporation Leyland bus, a 1937 TD4c or 1938 TD5c, is on route 2 from Harrison Drive to Seacombe. These were the first Wallasey buses to carry the Metropolitan Cammell (Birmingham) body and the progenitors of the standard Wallasey bus for the mid-20th century. Buses of this design continued to be built until 1951 and were seen on the streets of Wallasey right through from 1937 to 1973. *Allan Clayton, Online Transport Archive*

Top right Some of the sandstone cottages of the old village street survive on the left of this picture of **WALLASEY VILLAGE**, looking south from the corner of Green Lane; they lasted till 1966. There is a recessed parade of shops, of which we can see Miss Elizabeth Reid's wool shop and George Eccles, greengrocer. Over the roof can be seen the spire of the red-brick Presbyterian Church of 1899, and the Birkenhead & District Co-op grocery shop stands on the corner of Sandy Lane. Demolition had begun in 1950 on the last narrow section of the old village street, from Sandy Lane to Leasowe Road – small, grim, almost black sandstone cottages, mostly the homes of market gardeners – and most of those on the left or east side of the street had been cleared by the time of this photograph. The shops, from the right, are Doreen's (children's outfitter), the Sandy Café, F. Maddock (barber)

and the Wallasey Coal Company office. Across the side street, with Wirral Villas, are Clarence Waller (newsagent), the Phoenix Cinema (built 1951) and the Farmer's Arms public house. The car parked on the right is a 1938 Morris 8, and the van on the left is a 1940s Fordson 10. A motorcycle combination is parked in front of the van; this was a common means of travel for families who could not afford a car. *St Alban's series postcard*

Below The north end of Wallasey's main street is viewed from the corner of Grove Road (left) and the entrance to the forecourt of Wallasey Grove Road station (right). Behind the camera Harrison Drive leads over the railway bridge and the grass-covered dunes down to the beach. The corner building on the left was the former Grove Temperance Hotel with 90

bedrooms and a café. At the time of this 1955 photograph the hotel had closed and the café was Reece's; in 1957 the first floor became the Melody Inn Club, with a dance hall and restaurant. The succession of white sun blinds over the shop fronts substitutes the former cast-iron and glass colonnade that stretched the full length of this three-storey block. Martin's Bank in Edwardian-baroque of 1909 stands on the corner of Groveland Road (right), and the signs on the leaning lamp post point to Wallasey Grove Road station and Wallasey Golf Club. All the street lamps in this view are mounted on the former tramway traction poles that held the span wires from which the electric wires were suspended, and the post on the right leaned outward to take the tension of the overhead rigging on this wide open space where the tramway turned the corner from Wallasey Village into Grove Road. *Valentine's postcard*

Above This 1946 Wallasey bus, standing in **GROVE ROAD, WALLASEY**, in 1954, was one of the 130 buses of this classic Wallasey design built by the Metropolitan Cammell Carriage & Wagon Company at Birmingham on Leyland Titan chassis between 1937 and 1951, and seen on the streets of Wallasey till 1973. This was one of the 21 buses in the 1946 batch on Titan PD1 chassis, and was No 93 in the fleet; this stock remained in service till 1957-60. No 93 was sold in 1959 to a dealer at Walmer Bridge and exported to Sarajevo in 1960 together with four other Wallasey buses of the same stock. It is seen here at the outer terminus of route 6 from Seacombe via King Street and Belvidere Road, and the buses turned round the roundabout at the junction with Warren Drive (off to the left). The number 6 was an obscure bus route, taking a tortuous course through back streets via Trafalgar Road, Serpentine Road, Martin's Lane, Grosvenor Street, Westminster Road, Mill Lane and Rullerton Road, and terminating here in this

quiet, high-class residential area a mile short of New Brighton. The route originally ran to New Brighton in 1931 but was cut back to Grove Road in 1933. Route 6 had a chequered history of diversions and extensions till closure in 1965, but settled down to the route described above throughout the period from 1947 till 1960 with extensions to New Brighton or Derby Bathing Pool on fine summer weekends.

Below **WARREN DRIVE, WALLASEY**, the main road from Wallasey into New Brighton, is viewed from the floral roundabout at the junction with Grove Road. The road was built over a rabbit warren between the heath and the dunes in 1880 and lined with large, detached houses, becoming the most salubrious address in Wallasey island. There was a Warren station on the railway in the grassy dunes halfway between New Brighton and Wallasey from 1888 to 1915; it was on the east side of Sea Road but the access road was off the apex of the bend

in Warren Drive at Warren Point. However, the Liverpool businessmen who lived on Warren Drive changed their allegiance from the railway to the electric tramcar and the ferry from 1902, and in latter years Warren station was mainly used by golfers for the Warren Municipal Golf Links. In the 1950s the businessmen travelled by the number 16 bus and made up the bowler-hat-and-briefcase brigade that paraded around the promenade deck on the Seacombe Ferry.

A breeze rustled the leaves of the trees of the wide, empty road on this fresh, sunny morning in August 1961. This and the singing of the birds and the distant sound of the Corporation's cream and green Shelvoke & Drewry dustcart were the only sounds on the A554 at this time of the morning. The houses on the left, the west side of the road, looked out over the grass-covered dunes to the Irish Sea and the Welsh mountains.

Above The houses on Warren Drive and the steeple of the Presbyterian Church on Ennerdale Drive can be seen across the grass-covered dunes of **HARRISON PARK, WALLASEY**, on the shore side of the town. Harrison Park and Harrison Drive, leading to Wallasey Beach, were developed on land given to the borough in 1896 by the Harrison family in memory of James Harrison of Wallasey, co-founder of T. & J. Harrison Ltd, the Liverpool shipping line, who died in 1891. The park was developed among the dunes, with a bowling green, cricket pitch and tennis courts, and the natural landscaping of this informal park makes it a favourite spot for family picnics and for children

romping over the hills. The Warren Municipal Golf Links lie between Harrison Park and Warren Drive. *F. Frith postcard, by permission of The Francis Frith Collection*

Below The wide, windswept promenade of **KING'S PARADE, WALLASEY**, built in 1934-39, is retained by a huge, ugly, concrete sea wall with a massive parapet that blocks the view of the sea to promenaders and forms a channel along the foot of the wall that cuts off access to the beach from the steps in the wall at intervals. The parapet has recesses along its full length that contained slatted wooden seats facing inland. The dual carriageway along this extension of King's Parade west of the Red Noses has been used as a racecourse for cycles, motorcycles and motorcars. There was a summer bus service along here, the 19, from New Brighton Pier to Wallasey Beach, from 1939 to 1961, then to Derby Bathing Pool till 1967; a stop flag is seen left of the lamp post in this 1954 view. The land reclaimed by the new sea wall, inland of the promenade, was intended for hotels, flats, public gardens and other seaside amenities but, with the demise of New Brighton as a holiday resort, the land has not been developed and these expansive sunken greens are a greater amenity as recreational open space. Beyond the greens are the silhouettes of the grass-covered sandhills and St Nicholas's Church (left), built in 1910-11, serving the north end of Wallasey. Like the land for Harrison Drive and Harrison Park, the church was funded by the Harrison family as a memorial to James Harrison, of Wallasey, the ship-owner.

LIVERPOOL

Liverpool is closer to the sea, both physically and spiritually, than any other large port in Great Britain. Its 7-mile line of docks along the Mersey bank ends where the river enters the Irish Sea and the city centre is only 3 miles up-river. The Mersey is half a mile wide in front of the city centre and widens to 1 mile where it flows into the sea between Bootle and New Brighton so that Liverpool looks out on the grey horizon and the comings and goings of ships to and from all parts of the world. In its heyday, passenger liners tied up at the half-mile-long floating landing stage within a stone's throw of the great and noble shipping offices, while cargo-liners and freighters to and from the southern docks, Birkenhead, Garston, Bromborough, Ellesmere Port and Manchester, paraded past the city centre. The name of Liverpool was the port of registry on the sterns of liners and freighters all over the world. It was the port of departure for emigrants to the New World and, as the home port for British troopships till 1958, it was the scene of many happy homecomings.

Up here among the gulls in the salty air, 180 miles north-west of London, was a self-centred northern metropolis that was the second most important port in Britain and the country's chief port in the trans-Atlantic trade. Cotton was its staple import and the Cotton Exchange in Old Hall Street was the leading cotton market in Europe. Together with Birkenhead it was also the largest grain-milling centre this side of the Atlantic. Liverpool was a city of superlatives: it had the largest clock dials in England, the largest warehouse, the largest cold storage and the largest floating crane in Britain, the longest floating structure and the longest underwater tunnel in the world, and St James's was the largest cathedral with the largest organ in Britain and the highest and heaviest peal of bells in the world.

The largest floating structure was the 2,533-foot-long landing stage that was the berth for ocean liners, Irish Sea ferries and Mersey ferries at all states of the 31-foot tidal range in the Mersey estuary. The largest clock dials were the 25-foot

faces of Great George on the fore and aft clock towers of the 295-foot-tall, black Liver Building that dominated the Mersey scene. The Liver Building is one of a trinity of architectural masterpieces on the waterfront behind the landing stage, together with the megalithic, Italianate head office of the famous Cunard Steamship Line and the domed, classical palace of the Dock Board. The liners at the landing stage with the waterfront trinity behind was the image of Liverpool in most people's minds and the vision we had as we steamed into Liverpool on the ferry from Seacombe close past the liners at the stage on our port bow.

The sounds of engine room telegraphs, churning water, tightening ropes and clattering gangways gave way to the cries of the newsvendors calling 'Echo, Express!' or 'Express and Echo!'. Appropriately, these cries echoed down the covered bridges to the landing stage as we bent our backs into the climb up the inclined bridges, the gradient depending on the state of the tide. The newsvendors were silhouetted in the top portals, which gradually revealed the size and splendour of the great buildings as we emerged on the wide, windy open space of George's Pier Head, the central tram terminus atop the river wall at the focal point of the city. We had entered Liverpool by the front door.

Pier Head was the exciting hub of Merseyside, animated by the world's shipping and what was probably the world's busiest tramway centre. 'PIER HEAD' was the legendary destination on most city-bound tramcars, but the vast tramway system, which was the pride of Liverpool in the 1930s with its modern cars and miles of reserved tracks, now suffered from a backlog of maintenance from six years of war and was in demise as, line by line, it was being replaced with motorbuses over the period from 1948 to 1957. Many of the tramcars were still matt black or dingy green with soot ingrained in the paintwork from lack of cleaning during the war, but the large fleet of cars was gradually being repainted and trams still dominated the Pier Head and the city streets in 1950.

The tramways were integrated into the fabric of the city, the rails bedded into the granite setts, the overhead electric rigging hung from iron rosettes on the walls of the buildings. The rising and ebbing hum of electric traction motors, the hiss of air brakes and the ring of steel on steel: the ever-present sound of the ubiquitous trams was the symphony of the city, which seemed strangely empty when the trams had gone.

From the deep, dark, bomb-scarred canyons of Water Street, James Street and Chapel Street, the tramcars emerged on to Pier Head with their trolleys sparking on the great web of electric wires against the sky, suspended from the lamp posts, and their trolley ropes billowing out behind in the wind. They lumbered through the complex of tracks to the river wall and jerked to a halt with a clatter and a hiss of brakes, then shunted and shuffled around three terminal loops with double tracks on the riverside loading bays beside a rambling, wooden waiting shed. A departure board (briefly recorded in the film *Waterfront*) listed the destinations of the cars from the three loops: the north loop for lines north, the middle loop for lines east and the south loop for lines south. Those from the north loop were destined for such romantic-sounding place names as Seaforth, Litherland and Fazakerley, written in large capitals in the side window destination screens. The whole of Liverpool was our oyster and a ride on any one of these lines was a memorable voyage through a fantastic city of contrasts.

We mounted the two steps in the wide doorway to the spacious vestibule that doubled as the conductor's platform and the motorman's cab on these doubled-ended vehicles. There was a third step into the lower saloon, which was thus well elevated above the street, or we clambered up the curving staircase to the top deck. The interior of the older standard cars was a veritable museum of woodwork and brasswork. From the top deck we looked down on the roofs of the passing buses. The height of the car combined with the large windows, which instilled a feeling of riding in a glasshouse, and the slender-looking tracks far below, generated an exciting feeling of insecurity in this 11-year-old boy, fresh from the tram-forsaken Cheshire bank. I used to wonder if the gaunt old four-wheelers would stay on the rails as

they rocked and rolled along and picked their way through the network of tracks with grooves cut in the road surface at junctions where the flanged wheels had derailed. Tramcars overhung their trucks fore and aft, giving a delayed response to bends in the tracks, and I could never be quite sure whether the car in which I was riding was taking the bend or not, but these heavy, railbound vehicles were surefooted and reliable in ice, snow and fog. Despite their age and condition, the bogie cars fairly bowled along smoothly and quietly and gave a superior and safer ride than the more modern buses that were usurping their routes.

WATER STREET

The top deck of the car arriving or loading on Pier Head gave passengers a grandstand view of shipping on the river and, as the car turned off Pier Head into the broad, dark canyon of Water Street between the Liver and Cunard Buildings, the gleaming ribbons of steel led alluringly through a dramatic cityscape. Water Street, Dale Street, William Brown Street and London Road were the main axis of Liverpool. A well-travelled friend from Amsterdam said he had never seen so many large, architecturally impressive buildings in close succession as when I took him on a walk through Liverpool.

The vista through the canyon from Pier Head into the city had shades of New York and Chicago in the 1930s, walled in by towering, ornate, stone buildings and crossed by the girders of the Liverpool Overhead Railway spanning the street behind the Pier Head buildings. The Overhead Railway was the first electric elevated railway in the world and vintage, wooden electric trains, dating from 1893, carrying dockers, seamen, clerks and sightseers along the 7-mile line of docks, rumbled overhead across the street on frequent headways. The line ran along a ruddy-brown iron and steel colonnade 16 feet above the tracks of the dock goods railway alongside the dock road, and sometimes our tramcar had to give right of way to a quaint saddle-tank dockside steam engine with a long train of trucks and vans, ambling along behind a man walking with a red flag. Paradoxically, the flagman was a regulation on the Liverpool dock railways but not in Birkenhead or

Wallasey, where the dock railways were more intimately mixed up with the roads. The tramcar clumped and clanked across the dock railway tracks and its trolley ducked under the Overhead girders beside the complicated wooden structure of the elevated Pier Head station behind the Liver Building.

As we emerged from the shadow of the Overhead we crossed the wide, granite-paved dock road, busy with motor lorries, steam lorries and steaming teams of great draught horses pulling wagons loaded with sacks, barrels, boxes, bundles or machinery, usually led by their drivers in cloth caps and leather aprons walking in front. As the dock road passed through the city centre at this point, two blocks of six-storey brick warehouses and offices with stone arcading around the ground floors occupied the middle of the road behind the Cunard and Dock Buildings from Water Street to James Street with dock road traffic passing along both sides. This section of the dock road rejoiced in the name of Goree Piazzas (formerly Goree Causeway)*. The arcaded block, largely gutted by fire in the 1941 blitz and partly in ruins, towered on our right as the tramcar lumbered across the dock road.

To our left, behind the Liver Building, the parish church of St Nicholas stood out starkly with its soot-black tower and flying Gothic spire standing tall above the embanked churchyard behind its high stone retaining wall above the dock road on the corner of Chapel Street. A chapel and churches have stood on this site since 1355, dedicated to St Nicholas, the patron saint of seafarers. For centuries the churchyard wall was the river wall and the church tower was the chief landmark on the waterfront of old Liverpool. The church tower we see today was built in 1811-15, 120 feet tall, topped with a 60-foot buttressed, lantern spire. The nave was destroyed by a bomb in the 1940 Christmas air raids and rebuilt in 1949-52 in matching Gothic stonework. The old and new parts of the church were as distinguishable as black from white, for those were, respectively, the colours of the stonework of the steeple and the nave. St Nicholas's Parish Church bears a remarkable resemblance to the 14th- and 15th-century St Nicholas Cathedral in Newcastle-upon-Tyne.

The cast-iron street nameplate on the churchyard wall reads GEORGE'S DOCK GATES, which is the name of this short stretch of the dock road between Goree Piazzas and New Quay. All the ground from the dock road to the river wall is reclaimed land as the docks were built out into the river rather than dug out of the river bank. Twentieth-century man would not have recognised Liverpool waterfront from the Mersey in 1895, except for the tower of St Nicholas's Church, and he would not have been impressed by the frontage of dock walls and grim warehouses. George's Dock, dating from 1771, lay in front of the city centre, its piers and swing bridges across the dock entrances giving access to the riverside ferry landings on George's Pier Head. The Goree warehouses stood alongside George's Dock.

The transformation of the waterfront came in the years 1896 to 1916. Norman Shaw's noble White Star Line office was built at the foot of James Street in 1896-98, the splendid Tower Buildings in 1906 on the site of the old fortified waterfront tower, and George's Dock was drained and partly filled in about 1900 to provide the foundations and cellars of the Liver, Cunard and Dock Buildings, erected between 1903 and 1916, by which time the waterfront presented a very different image from only 20 years earlier. The transformation did not end there for, as we head up Water Street, the most impressive buildings in this street were put up in the 1920s: the India Building, the Bank of British West Africa and the head office of Martin's Bank.

As we mount the inclines of Water Street, James Street or Chapel Street, we climb the slopes of the original Mersey bank above the old tidemark along the inland side of the dock road. As we ascend Water Street, the profile of the Town Hall and its classical portico jut out more than halfway across the summit of the street at its junction with Castle Street and Dale Street in a piece of cityscape

* The Goree of Goree Piazzas is the Manx name for Godred, the name of four of the Norse rulers of Man and the Hebrides in the 10th to 13th centuries, hence the name of the four former successive Manx ships named King Orry, pronounced 'Kin-gorry' in Liverpool. Goree was also the name of an island off Dakar, Senegal, used to corral natives captured for the west African slave trade and awaiting transhipment to the Americas.

theatre that is a superb foil to the continuous line of Water Street and Dale Street. The carriageway curves around it in a deferential bow-shaped curve at the T-junction with Castle Street, and this venerable Palladian forum with its lantern dome, Corinthian portico and rusticated arcading forms a dramatic termination of the view along Castle Street.

OLD LIVERPOOL

This is the fourth Town Hall here – or the third Town Hall of 1754 remodelled after the fire of 1795 – and this junction was the first market place and centre of the old village and town of Liverpool. Thirteenth-century kings made Liverpool a port for shipping troops and stores to Ireland, fortified it with a castle and a wall, granted freedom of tenure to the serfs, invited settlers to take up tenancies and gave Liverpool borough status. From records dated 1356 and 1525 we know it had a mayor, 12 (self-elected) councillors, bailiffs and by-laws, but it was only a village or a small town in the Parish of Walton (now a suburb of the city), the Hundred of West Derby (another suburb) and the diocese of Lichfield and, later, of Chester. HM Customs described it as 'a creek in the port of Chester'.

Liverpool was under siege three times during the Civil War (1642-45), the Castle changing hands each time, from Royalists to Parliamentarians to Royalists to Parliamentarians, within the first two years.

Trade boomed and the population swelled from the second half of the 17th century, but Liverpool was still only a small medieval town with seven streets. Castle Street, High Street (formerly Juggler Street) and Old Hall Street ran along the top of the ridge above the river. Fishing boats and coastal traders unloaded on the shore at the foot of Water Street and Chapel Street (by the then chapel of St Nicholas) and took shelter in The Pool, a creek on the south and east sides of the old town (now Paradise Street, Whitechapel and Old Haymarket). Dale Street led inland across the dale of The Pool and a bridge carried the road on to Prescot for York and London. Tithebarn Street (formerly Moor Street) led to Walton church, Lancaster and Scotland.

This medieval Liverpool was transformed in the 18th century, when the Corporation began building docks and churches and partially widening some streets from public funds. As the port of Chester was silting up, Liverpool opened its first impounded dock in the mouth of The Pool in 1715 and filled in the creek. The disused castle was pulled down in 1717 to make way for St George's Church and a new market place. Liverpool was now a parish in its own right and several more Georgian-style parish churches were built, St Peter's giving the name to Church Street as the town began to spread across the line of the creek. Liverpool Corporation built ten parish churches in the 18th century.

Four more docks, Salthouse, George's, King's and Queen's, were built in the second half of the 18th century and Liverpool eclipsed Bristol as the chief port on the west coast and the second port of the realm after London. Dock construction, combined with the Industrial Revolution, saw the town grow threefold between 1760 and 1815 and the population fourfold in the same period with immigrants. Liverpool was now the most densely populated town in England and notorious for its slum alleys, courtyards and cellars. Its main streets were still narrow, unpaved, dirty and unlit – but very picturesque in paintings of the period with all the old buildings and bow-windowed shops.

Long-distance stagecoach services are first recorded in 1766, and by the turn of the century between 70 and 80 coaches a day terminated at the hostelries in Dale Street and Castle Street. The wealthier merchants created streets and squares of Georgian elegance in a belt around the city and erected country mansions on the hill above Everton village. By the time of the first national census in 1801 the population of Liverpool was 77,653, crammed into an area between Leeds Street and Parliament Street and extending inland to Rodney Street and Richmond Row. Lime Street, then Limekiln Lane, was on the edge of open country and 28 whirling windmills stood along the skyline on the slopes and ridge behind the town right down to the sandhills along the north shore.

Picturesque Liverpool of this period was notorious not only for its slums but also for congestion in the docks, privateers, press gangs, slave traders and for wreckers along its western approaches (Wirral and Wales). Liverpool was proud of its privateers, which were privately owned ships equipped with guns and commissioned by the Admiralty to capture the merchant ships and cargoes of any hostile nations, such as France and America. Press gangs terrorised civilians and merchant seamen by forceful recruitment to the Army and Navy. Slave traders took exports to Africa, slaves to the West Indies and brought cotton to Liverpool from 1770. Wreckers lured ships on to the sandbanks with bonfires, robbed the survivors and plundered the cargoes.

Those evil days were only put behind us with the reforms, developments and civilising influences of the 19th century. The slave trade was abolished in 1807 but privateering went on till 1856. Just as 18th-century Liverpool transformed the older town, so 19th-century Liverpool almost totally eclipsed the 18th-century town. All the old craftsmen, the shipwrights in oak, the potters and the watchmakers, were ousted by dock construction, new industries and overcrowding by immigrants, mainly starving Irish, who gave Liverpolitans a new accent and humour. The old shipbuilding yards along the riverfront were shut down as the docks spread north and south. Liverpool had 14 potteries employing 2,000 men in the 18th century but they had all closed by 1815. Another 2,000 had been employed in watchmaking.

The last relics of old Liverpool, the waterfront Tower of 1406, once a residence of the Earls of Derby, latterly a prison, and the 16th-century Tithe Barn in Tithebarn Street, came down in the 1820s, when the Corporation embarked on a massive programme of street works: widening, paving and gas lighting under the supervision of John Foster, Borough Surveyor and Architect (1824-35). He was an architect of the classical tradition and 19th-century Liverpool was laid out with wide streets, squares, crescents and classical buildings. The original dock was filled in to become Canning Place and the site of the new Customs House, which Foster designed in the classical style with a lantern dome to complement the Town Hall at the opposite end of Castle Street. The town centre was transformed with the great cultural edifices around William Brown Street (formerly Shaw's Brow). But the slums of the old town remained.

From the departure of the first steam train to Manchester in 1830 and the first trans-Atlantic steamship to New York in 1838 Liverpool developed into the great ocean terminus for North America and a vast, industrial city supplying the marine industry and processing its imports such as grain and sugar. The first steamship had appeared on the Mersey on the Liverpool-Runcorn ferry in 1815 but the transition from sail to steam was slow and cautious. Clarence Dock (1830) was the first dock designated for steamships – at a safe distance from the town in case of boiler explosions – and sailing ships outnumbered steamships in the port until about 1900.

Samuel Cunard came to Liverpool from Halifax, Nova Scotia, on the pioneer trans-Atlantic paddle-steamer *Liverpool* from New York in 1839 to start his British & North American Royal Mail Steam Packet Company at Liverpool in 1840 with the PS *Britannia*. This became the famous Cunard Line, which cut the passage to Boston from 14 days to eight days by 1863. The Oceanic Steam Navigation Company's White Star Line competed with Cunard on the New York service from 1871 and the two companies merged in 1934 with the largest and fastest luxury liners afloat, on services from Liverpool and Southampton to New York.

Liverpool Corporation had built most of the docks, from Brunswick to Sandon, lighthouses at Bidston and Leasowe and the first observatory, at Waterloo Dock (1843), to predict tides and set chronometers, and had taken over the beginnings of the Birkenhead docks before handing over the ownership and operation of the port to the new Mersey Docks & Harbour Board in 1857.

The worst of the old town slums were cleared in the second half of the 19th century as new streets of barrack-like terraced houses with clean water supply and sewers urbanised the surrounding countryside from Dingle to Kirkdale, covering Edge Hill and Everton on the way. The streets of terraced houses, the warehouses and the docks continued north into neighbouring Bootle, which was transformed from a village to a borough in 40 years.

Liverpool emerged into the 20th century with some dignity and pride, but it was a city of contrasts and that was no compliment because it still had more square miles of mean streets of depressing drabness, poverty and squalor than any other city in England, and many of the old slum alleys were not cleared till the 1920s and '30s. Relying as it did on international trade, Liverpool suffered twice the national average rate of unemployment in the inter-war recession. The Mersey Tunnel construction in 1926-34 provided some unemployment relief and a direct road to Birkenhead, eclipsing the vehicular ferries.

The city also suffered successive sleepless nights of hell in the May 1941 air raids during the Second World War. There were nights when the city and docks seemed to be burning from end to end and the people emerged from their homes and shelters each morning to ghastly scenes of devastation. Forty per cent of the houses in Liverpool and Bootle were destroyed or damaged in that one month, leaving 51,000 people homeless. Craters in the streets dislocated water, gas, electricity, telephone and tram services. The crew of a fire engine were killed when it plunged into a crater in Roe Street in the 1940 Christmas blitz. By war's end in 1945 Liverpool and Bootle had lost 3,056 people killed. Another 5,574 were injured. Liverpool also lost many of its churches and fine buildings, notably the old Customs House and the Cotton Exchange, and hardly a building in the city escaped damage. But Liverpool never lost its spirit; firefighting, rescue and recovery work continued and the docks were kept busier than ever before.

After the war Liverpool looked very much like the post-war Vienna we saw in the film *The Third Man* in 1949 with noble buildings standing amid bombed sites and piles of rubble, but life went on almost as if nothing had happened. The 35 years since its Edwardian heyday had been bad times. Liverpool never looked back. Now was a time of recovery and almost full employment, of National Health, ration books and cheerful chin-upmanship. Trade in the docks continued to rise to new records and the troopships and passenger liners returned to the Landing Stage. At the 1951 census the combined population of Liverpool, Litherland and Bootle was 886,031.

St George's, St Peter's and all the other 18th-century parish churches were lost in the 19th and early 20th century commercial development of the city centre or in the war, leaving only the 1815 tower of the original church of St Nicholas on the waterfront. The beautiful Queen Anne-style Bluecoat School for poor children (1717-25) in School Lane is now the oldest building in the city centre, and the elegant Town Hall, by John Wood the younger of Bath in 1749-54, is the second oldest building.

SHOPPING, COMMERCE AND CULTURE

The Town Hall now stands at the heart of the commercial district, and at the other end of Castle Street the Queen Victoria Monument stands on the site of St George's Church and the former Castle. The Empress Queen, under the umbrella of a classical dome on columns, was now encircled by tramcars on the Castle Street terminal loop amid an urban desert, as the surviving Georgiana of St George's Crescent, South Castle Street and the south side of Lord Street had been bombed in the war. Beneath Her Majesty was a suitably splendid suite of Edwardian lavatories for the gentlemen of the surrounding offices. Also in the commercial district, the tram tracks through Victoria Street and Chapel Street passed both sides of underground lavatories with steps descending from railed islands in the middle of the road, perhaps for the convenience of tram drivers. The underground lavatories in the wide part of Victoria Street were surrounded by the stalls, boxes and vans of the busy street market for wholesale fruit and vegetables, which had been bombed out of its market hall.

If you walked into the city up James Street and down Lord Street you would be distracted by barrow boys and street entertainers on the bombed sites. The whole south side of Lord Street was flattened in the 1940-41 blitz and remained open wasteland until rebuilt in the late 1950s and early '60s, and this area was a nest of fruit and vegetable sellers, disabled ex-servicemen selling boxes of matches and novelties, tramps playing violins, jugglers and, best of all, the escapologists, who, bound up in sacks and chains, drew large crowds to witness their escape within 3 minutes.

Lord Street led into the shopping centre of the city with its large department stores like Bunney's in Whitechapel, Henderson's, C&A Modes and Bon Marché in Church Street, George Henry Lee's in Basnett Street, Owen Owen's in Clayton Square,

Blackler's in Bold Street, Lewis's in Renshaw Street and T. J. Hughes in London Road. We could rest our feet or dodge in from the rain in the news theatres, the Tatler Cinema in Church Street and the Liverpool News Theatre in Clayton Square, to sit through the continuous hourly film programme of newsreels and cartoons in the days before television.

The seven streets of the old town are the commercial centre, for shipping, banking and insurance. The dark canyon of Dale Street reaches inland from the Town Hall between towering, sombre office buildings in the variety of revival styles of the Victorian and Edwardian periods, notably by Charles Cockerell, Alfred Waterhouse and Francis Doyle for insurance companies. The golden cupolas of the Royal Insurance Building and the 200-foot clock steeple of the Municipal Buildings are the chief landmarks.

I remember my first journey into Liverpool, by tramcar from Pier Head via Dale Street in 1949. The Pier Head, the Overhead, the dock traffic, the Goree Piazzas, and the architectural dignity of Water Street and Dale Street were a succession of assaults on the senses of this impressionable Southern boy of 11, but the greatest surprise lay in store at the east end of Dale Street. The curtain of buildings drew aside to reveal the most breathtaking theatrical cityscape I have ever seen, like a set for one of Cecil B. De Mille's epic classics of the cinema screen. Here in the city centre was a vast arena of gardens, statues and free-standing columns against a backdrop of gigantic classical buildings with Corinthian colonnades, all scowling black with soot.

This was Old Haymarket with St John's Gardens and the Mersey Tunnel entrance. The gardens were formerly St John's Church and churchyard, which, together with many old houses and shops in Old Haymarket and Shaw's Brow (now William Brown Street), were cleared to create this wide open space at the heart of the city with roads and tramways radiating in seven directions. The scene was crawling with tramcars that looked small and slow-moving in these broad acres and against the large scale of the buildings. The theatrical quality of this cityscape is enhanced by the contours of the dale around the head of the former creek, The Pool, and the way the buildings have been arranged to catch the light and to close off and

disclose further monumental open spaces beyond the immediate view from Dale Street.

The Technical College, the Brown Library and Museum, the Picton Reference Library, the Walker Art Gallery and County Sessions House are ranged up the slope on the north side of the arena, facing south into the sun. The 500-foot-long St George's Hall stretches across the top of the slope on the east side with the sun catching both flanks, morning and afternoon, and a south-facing portico. This great, central, open space is so vast and has so many ramifications that we cannot see it all from any one viewpoint. In the view from Dale Street, St George's Hall appears as the backdrop of the scene but in fact holds centre stage, fronting on to a stepped plateau with more monuments on the Lime Street side with a wide, triangular open space at each end.

In all its black grandeur, St George's Hall, that monarch of 19th-century classicism, was like Siegfried's funeral music set in stone, reaching a climax in its rich interior. It was built in 1838-54 to house an assembly hall, assize courts and a concert theatre. It was designed by Harvey Elmes in his early 20s, but this genius died at 33 under the strain of supervising the construction and his great work was completed under Charles Cockerell, whose classical work we see in Castle Street and Dale Street. The entrance is under the long, Corinthian colonnade fronting Lime Street, not through the grand portico on the south end. The assembly hall, 169 feet long, with its soaring, Romanesque arches and barrelled and coffered ceiling 82 feet high, its red granite columns, marble balustrading, brass doors and sunken tiled floor, is remarkable for the richness of its colour and gilding. The architectural experience is enhanced by the sound of the 8,000-pipe Willis organ, one of the largest in the world. The north apse houses an enchanting, semi-circular concert theatre with a domed skylight, designed by Cockerell. The total composition is magnificent.

The colonnaded north apse of St George's Hall complements the colonnaded rotunda of the Picton Reference Library opposite. The rotunda nicely rounds off the bend into the fork junction with Islington (formerly Islington Row). As we pass between the two buildings on our ascent of William Brown Street the scene opens out again into a triangular junction with Islington and Commutation Row, more classical buildings – the Walker Art Gallery and the County Sessions House – come into view, marching on up the slope of Islington, and the Steble Fountain and the Wellington Monument (Liverpool's equivalent of Nelson's Column) stand in the triangle.

Lime Street and St George's Plateau form a broad swath, with statuesque monuments, along the east side of the great hall with its long entrance colonnade. Its south-facing portico, like a Greek temple, towers above a massive flight of steps and a cliff-like retaining wall overlooking another wide, triangular junction at the top of the slope of St John's Lane. In our 1950 perambulation this triangle, St George's Place, was a tramway station with island platforms, and there was often a crowd of people standing oblivious of the tramcars and motor traffic passing close by on three sides – they were concentrating on the regular seaside-style Punch & Judy show in a small canvas booth of red and white stripes, which was a nice foil to the mighty portico above.

The immense glazed arch of one of the two broad, elliptical spans of Lime Street station trainshed, on the east side of the street opposite St George's Place, terminated the view up St John's Lane. The station was half hidden in a recessed gap between the North Western Hotel and the Royal Hotel on the street frontage. Lime Street was the main railway terminus in Liverpool, formerly of the London & North Western Railway, its rivals being the former Cheshire Lines into Central station in Ranelagh Street (which closed in 1972) and the old Lancashire & Yorkshire Railway into Exchange station in Tithebarn Street (which closed in 1977). The line into Lime Street was an 1836 extension of the pioneer Liverpool & Manchester Railway of 1830 from Edge Hill and a dramatic way to enter the city, second only to the approach by river to the Pier Head.

From Edge Hill the railway plunged down a four-track cutting between sheer walls of soot-blackened sandstone, covered with large patches of moss and dripping water. As we descended, the walls of the chasm rose to a height of 80 feet and deep bridges and tunnels bearing numerous back streets over the top of the cutting came in an ever-quickening succession of graceful, lofty, black

stone arches until the railway seemed entombed in a long, gloomy cavern descending into some underworld like Niflheim in Norse mythology. The brakes went on and the flanges sounded like sawmills as we levelled out under the broad span of the twin-arch trainshed on massive cast-iron piers and we were in the smoky, echoing, twilight zone of Lime Street station. As we walked out of the ramped station entrance, blinking in the daylight, the view before us was enough to take the breath away from a stranger arriving in this northern metropolis for the first time. We were on the brink of that awesome, monumental open space in the centre of the city with wide streets and tramcars in all directions and the great, black buildings rising and falling in terraces on the contours. Down St John's Lane you could see the skyline of towers and cupolas of the commercial district stretching to the waterfront with the clock towers of the Liver Building towering overall.

The final phase of the development of this monumental open space in the centre of Liverpool came in 1926-34 with the clearance of old buildings in a triangle on one side of Old Haymarket, Manchester Street and the east end of Dale Street and the construction of the main entrance to the Mersey Tunnel. This modern construction lived up to its monumental setting in 1930s classical style but the portal, retaining walls and triumphal arches were in a contrasting white Portland stone. The tunnel entrance was lit by Art Deco, half-moon street lamps on tall, slender columns and a massive, fluted 60-foot lighting column of polished black granite, as a monument to its builders. The portal faces up William Brown Street to St George's Hall and a driver's first impression on emerging from the modern tunnel is that he has arrived in ancient Greece or Rome.

THE SEEDY SIDE

So far we have seen the noble face of Liverpool, but now that we have got accustomed to the grandeur of this setting we begin to perceive, in the shadows on the south side of Manchester Street and St John's Lane, the shady side of Liverpool. The grand portico of St George's Hall presided over seedy streets of decayed Regency and Victorian buildings on the slope below.

Once your tramcar left the main city centre framework of Tithebarn Street, Church Street and Lime Street, the image faded immediately as you headed into Vauxhall Road, Byrom Street, Islington, London Road, Brownlow Hill or Great George Street through the desolation of drab, grim streets of terraced houses, dingy corner taverns, pawnbrokers' shops, extensive bombed sites and many empty, condemned and boarded-up houses and shops that stretched for miles through the inner city slum belt before we reached the reserved grass tracks through the pleasant, sylvan, outer suburbs. In fact, the lines north through Everton, Kirkdale and Bootle never saw the end of the terraced houses before they reached their terminals at Seaforth, Litherland and Aintree, 3 miles north of the city centre.

One night in 1950, the eve of my return to boarding school, Dad took me on what, for me, was a treat. It was a mystery tour. We rode a pre-war Birkenhead bus from Wallasey to Woodside, a ferry steamer to Liverpool, a standard tram to Litherland and back to Pier Head, a ferry steamer to Seacombe and a Wallasey bus back home. (How many of us wish we could do that now?) Dad knew I wanted to ride a tram to Litherland because of the name with its connotations in my mind with the sinister sound of the zither in Harry Lime's post-war Vienna. Dad worked in Exchange Buildings by day and came home to Wallasey by ferry and bus for tea, so we went to Litherland in the evening. On Pier Head we boarded a suitably gaunt, soot-black Standard tramcar on line 16 and headed up Chapel Street. It was as well we made the journey in the dark because it was much more atmospheric. Dad had been told by his office colleagues that nobody travelled to Litherland by tram at night because it was likely to be ambushed; they all went by the Overhead Railway. We were the only passengers on the tramcar as it droned through Vauxhall Road and Commercial Road with the wet granite setts and tramlines gleaming ahead in the dim gas lights through this canyon of grim warehouses and derelict shops with a dingy tavern on almost every street corner. We were not ambushed in either direction and Litherland looked better in the dark; by day it did not look sinister at all.

Liverpool probably had more square miles of shabbiness, poverty and squalor than any other city in Britain but there was a certain quaintness I liked and they were not all slums. In the 1950s these 19th-century workers' barracks retained a Victorian character with their street gas lanterns, original Victorian street nameplates and iron bollards across the top of steep streets. The atmosphere was brightened by the lively and friendly character of the people with their quick-witted good humour, by housewives who whitewashed or scrubbed the doorsteps, and by children playing on the streets and bombed sites. The children perpetuated quite old, traditional games, chalked out on the footpaths, that had long died out in other parts of the country. Some of the streets and many of the bombed sites were reserved as children's playgrounds. The bombed sites and the steep streets of Everton, Edge Hill and Toxteth along the ridge at the back of the city also gave the denizens views over the terraced rooftops and the river to what must have seemed the promised land of Wirral and Wales.

GOTHIC REVIVAL AND GEORGIAN TWILIGHT

South of the city centre, the drab streets and run-down, late-Georgian tenements reached right up through Chinatown to the foot of St James's Cathedral, which crowns the ridge at this point, and this Wagnerian, neo-Gothic epic in red sandstone towered majestically over the steep, humble streets that dropped away below. Building began in 1904 with stone from Woolton quarry only 5 miles away. Construction progressed at the rate limited by funds, the high standard of stonemasonry required and a shortage of masons. The 1930s was the peak period of construction, with 187 men on site.

Work never stopped for the war – although the labour force was reduced to 35 – and the tower was completed and the transept on the north side opened in 1941, two months after Liverpool's worst blitz. The architect, Sir Giles Scott, laid the topmost stone on the last pinnacle of the tower. Despite the devastation all around, the huge hilltop Cathedral suffered only bomb blast to the west side. When workmen returned after the war there were 76 men on site by 1950 including 19 masons. The Cathedral was so vast that it was still only two-thirds towards completion in the 1950s, with the Lady Chapel, the chancel, the central tower and the transepts. Work had begun on the nave, which ended abruptly in a curtain wall. The Cathedral was then 450 feet long, but it was already the largest in Britain and the largest Anglican cathedral in the world, with a central tower soaring 347 feet above the street.

One firm of contractors, William Morrison & Son of Wavertree, worked on the job from the start till the firm closed down in 1968. The Cathedral Committee completed the work by direct labour over the next 10 years. The building finally extended 600 feet in length.

St George's Hall and St James's Cathedral are Liverpool's two architectural masterpieces and both were designed by architects in their early 20s in open competitions. Giles Scott was 23 when he won the design competition for the Cathedral, but, under the guiding light of the assessor, George Bodley, he revised his winning design during construction of the initial Lady Chapel into a quite different plan, boldly three-dimensional in form with a central tower flanked by twin transepts, owing more to Charles Mackintosh's unplaced design than Scott's own fussy original.

The Cathedral is even more awesome inside for its vaulted vastness, uncluttered with pillars, the broad arches, the warm glow of the sunlight through the tall, stained-glass windows on the red sandstone, picked out with white mortar, and the elegant stonecarving and woodcarving. Scott designed everything down to the hinges and door handles, and stayed with his masterpiece till he died in 1960 and was buried there, although he was a Roman Catholic. It makes one proud that this was 20th-century workmanship. To view the cavernous interior to the strains of the great organ is a moving experience. The Willis & Lewis organ is the largest cathedral organ in the world with 9,765 pipes, two manuals and 145 stops.

Outside again, we had a fine view from the top of the steps over the rooftops of the city to the river and, on the opposite bank, Birkenhead with its towering shipyard cranes, backed by the wooded ridges of the Wirral peninsula. That was the western prospect.

The Cathedral is founded on the red sandstone outcrop of St James's Mount. It towers like a fortress above the vast chasm of an old quarry on its east side that supplied the stone for much of 18th-century Liverpool and was now a forgotten necropolis of Liverpool's Victorians with soot-black gravestones, urns, obelisks, vaults and mausoleums in a jungle of trees and tall grass, and catacombs tunnelled into the cliff face of the quarry. The cemetery chapel was a small, soot-black, Greek temple (John Foster, 1829) perched dramatically atop the sheer north cliff on Upper Duke Street. Broad, well-graded ramps for horse-drawn funeral processions were built into the stone retaining wall on the east side, giving access from Hope Street, and a foot tunnel to the cemetery cuts through the rock face of the quarry from the corner of Upper Duke Street and St James Road.

Along the top of the east cliff of the quarry, facing the Cathedral, is a theatrical backdrop of the Regency, stone-colonnaded Gambier Terrace along Hope Street, the frontage of the surviving early-19th-century residential suburbs of the city. In the context of Victorian industrial Liverpool, the explorer can wander in dazed disbelief through this residential quarter of an earlier civilisation between Hope Street and Grove Street, Abercromby Square and Upper Parliament Street. It is a delightful oasis of streets and squares of terraced, red-brick, stuccoed and stone houses and occasional neo-Greek buildings in stone or stucco, but it is a Regency twilight zone, where the opposing forces of conservation and neglect strike an uneasy balance.

It was once the residential area of Liverpool professionals and merchants who preferred to live close to their business in the city on their doorstep and patronise its civic and cultural institutions rather than migrate west by steam ferry to the villa colonies of the Cheshire bank, as others did, to escape the spreading bustle, smoke and slums of the great seaport. These large houses were originally in single occupation of large families with servants but they eventually moved out as the spread of the slum streets surrounded what is now just a physical enclave of the age of elegance. By 1970 these houses were in multiple occupation by a mixture of professional classes, such as architects and surgeons, and by bohemian artists, poets, university students and prostitutes; the 'red light' district of Liverpool had moved out here from Lime Street. Sadly, many of the Regency houses on the fringe of the area had become the tenements of poorer people, probably with bad landlords, and were in a very neglected condition and an advanced state of decay.

Regency architecture was the final phase of the Georgian period between 1800 and 1830 and this Regency area of Liverpool is an extension of a late-18th-century Georgian area on the city side of Hope Street, between Mount Pleasant and Upper Duke Street. In the 18th century the Georgian houses of merchants, scholars and clerics covered the southern slopes of the city from Hope Street right down to Park Lane and Hanover Street, and by the early 19th century a belt of Georgian houses like these extended right around Liverpool. In the overcrowded industrial city of Victorian times those west of Roscoe Street and north of Mount Pleasant were later converted to tenements, workshops and warehouses and fell into decay or were demolished, leaving the area between Mount Pleasant and Upper Parliament Street as the legacy of Georgian Liverpool.

Rodney Street is the most perfectly preserved and fashionable street of this late-Georgian oasis and the best way to approach the Cathedral from the city centre. As the merchants, scholars and clerics moved out, the healing professions moved in. In the mid-20th century almost every house in Rodney Street was, like Harley Street in London, occupied by physicians, surgeons, dentists, gynaecologists, ophthalmologists, osteopaths, psychiatrists and other healing specialists with impressive strings of letters after their names on the brass plates. These houses, with their variety of columnar doorways, pediments, ornate fanlights and filigree iron balconies, were once the residences of the Liverpool aristocracy, merchant princes and distinguished figures. No 4 was the American consulate from 1790 to 1829. Henry Booth (1789-1869), founder secretary and treasurer of the Liverpool & Manchester Railway, lived at No 34; he was also the inventor of the screw coupling for railway rolling-stock. No 62 was the birthplace and boyhood home of William Gladstone (1809-98), Britain's greatest statesman and reformer. He was a Member of Parliament for 62 years and four times Prime Minister for a total

of 14 years between 1864 and 1894. The pioneer of radiology, Thurstan Holland (1863-1941), lived and worked at No 43. Liverpool's leading portrait photographer, Chambré Hardman (1898-1988), had his home and studio at No 59 from 1948 to 1988. His photographs of famous people, of landscapes and of Merseyside were studies in light and shadow like paintings.

North of Mount Pleasant, the Georgian area faded out into the typical, run-down, shabby, inner cityscape of Liverpool and the broad, bomb-scarred, littered road up Brownlow Hill. The top of the hill is crowned by the splendid Victorian Gothic main building of the University with a clock tower, by Alfred Waterhouse, which reminds me of St Pancras station by George Scott. Opposite the University lies the massive crypt of what was still, in 1950, to have been a monumental, classical, Roman Catholic Cathedral twice as large as St Paul's in London. Sir Edwin Lutyens (1869-1944), the most distinguished and prolific British architect, designed a massive composition of Romanesque arches, inspired by St Peter's Basilica in Rome, with 53 altars in a cruciform building and a dome 168 feet across, vaulting a central space 300 feet high. It would have been a third Liverpool masterpiece to rank with St George's Hall and St James's Cathedral but it was not to be. Work began in 1933 but was stopped by war in 1941, when the crypt was used as an air raid shelter. Building resumed in the mid-1950s under the direction of Adrian Scott, brother of the architect of St James's Cathedral, and the crypt with its three chapels opened in 1958. But this great work, which would have been larger than the Anglican Cathedral, was conceived too late. The cost and time-scale to complete this colossus were unacceptable in post-war Britain. In 1959 the Church put the Cathedral design out to competition, which resulted in a stark, circular, concrete cathedral in the style of a wigwam being erected in 1962-67 on an adjacent site incorporating the original crypt.

The classical crypt, in rusticated granite with Romanesque arches, was to be merely the plinth of the original cathedral and gives an impression of the style and heroic scale of the building Lutyens designed to be built in amber brick with grey granite string courses and architraves, and an all-granite interior. The completed crypt and the architect's model for the Cathedral, which was kept in the crypt from 1937 till 1975, are the only record of what is regarded as 'the greatest building that was never built'. Like Liverpool's transport relics and anything local, the model for Lutyens's cathedral has been relegated to storage to make way for exhibits of general or worldwide interest. However, the incomplete and damaged model in wood, 17 feet long and 11 feet tall, has been restored and completed by a team of seven craftsmen over the years 1992 to 2005, and we are told that all these local exhibits will eventually reappear on display in a new Museum of Liverpool Life, due to open on the site of Manchester Dock alongside Mann Island in 2010.

LAST CITY ECHOES

The granite setts cradled tram tracks, which disappeared over the crest of the hill on one of the many corridors of the great fan of lines of this network that once covered 98 miles of Liverpool streets. Brownlow Hill was on one of Liverpool's last two tram routes, the 40 from Pier Head to Page Moss. The other route was the 6A from Pier Head to Bowring Park via London Road. I hitch-hiked from Kent one weekend to ride them both one evening six weeks before the finale on 14 September, 1957. I never had the heart to attend 'last car' rites or tramway funerals; my last impression of a system had to be one of normal working service. I shall always remember my last tram ride through Liverpool, from Bowring Park to Pier Head, on that August evening in 1957. There were 66 tramcars left of a fleet that once numbered 784 and the two remaining routes were the last remnants of the great south Lancashire network that once extended from the Mersey to the Pennines. It was truly the end of an era.

The year 1957, Liverpool's 750th charter year, saw not only the end of the tramway system but also the demolition of the Overhead Railway and, with it, the last remnant of the Goree Piazzas. St John's Market in Great Charlotte Street was shutting down and 'Professor' Codman, the 60-year-old Punch & Judy man, was moved on from

his site in St George's Place, where he and his ancestors had been a Liverpool institution for 130 years, to make way for a car park. To me this was the end of an era of civilisation. I should never have returned to Liverpool to see its decline. I would prefer to remember it only as it was.

My last journey through Liverpool of that era was 5 miles of electric magic from Bowring Park to Pier Head. For the first mile and a half, the graceful green tramcar glided swiftly and quietly along reserved track in the middle of Broad Green Road, Bowring Park Road and Edge Lane Drive through the demure, middle-class suburbs. These dual carriageways with tramway reservations, laid with turf and bordered by hedges and trees, were designed and begun with great foresight by the City Engineer, John Brodie*, as early as 1914-15. Liverpool had 28 miles of these reservations, 28 per cent of the total route mileage, the last stretch being laid on the Kirkby extension in 1943-44. If they could have reached through the city centre to the Pier Head then the system might have survived into the modern tramway era.

We rumbled on to street track in the broad, granite-paved Edge Lane with its hurly-burly of diesel-fuming lorries and buses on the main road to Warrington and London. We passed the grandiose tramway depot and central workshops in Edge Lane, built in 1928 in classical red brick and Portland stone, where Liverpool Corporation built all its own tramcars as it had done previously at Lambeth Road works. Edge Lane was said to be the finest tramcar works in Britain. We could usually see some vintage Standard cars and work cars on the sidings in the yard.

From the brow of Edge Hill the city descended to the river in streets broad and narrow and wide open spaces in a series of dramatic effects enhanced by the contours of the ridges. In contrast to the spacious, sylvan suburbs, we entered the inner city slum belt on single tracks through one-way streets down narrow, dingy canyons of 19th-century terraces and tenements on a steep slope. We emerged from the dark slum streets into the lights of London Road shops and the monumental, dramatic grandeur of Lime Street and St George's

---

* John Brodie (1858-1934) was Liverpool City Engineer from 1898 to 1926. Besides pioneering dual carriageways with tramway reservations, he also invented football goal nets, first used in 1890, was a pioneer in the use of prefabricated housing and was joint design engineer for the Mersey Tunnel.

Plateau with a red glow effectively silhouetting the colonnade of the great St George's Hall as we glided past it down Lime Street. The steel lines, shining in the light of the street lamps and the shop windows, went winding ahead down through the almost empty streets. In the relative quiet of the night city I could hear the regular, gentle boom-boom of the trolley passing under each joint in the overhead wire. The dark windows of the offices above the shops slid by, level with the upper saloon of the tramcar.

On the final lap we nosed up Lord Street to mount the ridge of the old town by the river, hammered discordantly over the junction by the Queen Victoria Monument and swept smoothly and silently like a ghost down the last decline to the riverside. Crossing the empty dock road – where horse waggons and steam lorries could still be seen in daytime – the tramcar just fitted under the steel superstructure of the disused but extant Overhead Railway, simultaneously clanging across the dock railway lines that ran along underneath. Finally we passed alongside the great, domed Dock Building and swung round the bend on to the Pier Head. The power was knocked off and the tramcar lumbered and slumped to a halt with a gasp of air from the brakes. As I walked away towards the ferry landing stage, I turned and looked at the lit tramcar standing empty and alone against the backdrop of grey buildings and black night sky as another tramcar lumbered off into the gloomy canyons of the city, its trolley flashing in the darkness. The street lights glinted on the web of overhead wires and all was silent but for the newsvendors calling 'Last City Echo!' and the occasional sound of ships' hooters wafting in the wind off the dark river. The ferry steamer slipped stealthily from the landing stage and the lights of Liverpool waterfront receded astern in the enveloping, stygian blackness.

LIVERPOOL FROM SEACOMBE: In 1956 the Wallasey ferry steamer *Wallasey* of 1927, on passage from Seacombe, approaches Liverpool's famous waterfront, dominated by the Royal Liver Building, with the Canadian Pacific liner TSS *Empress of Scotland* (644 feet, 26,313 gross tons) berthed at the landing stage. The liner was launched from Fairfield's yard at Govan in 1929 as the *Empress of Japan* and made her maiden voyage on service from Liverpool to Quebec in 1930. She was renamed in 1942 while serving as a troopship during the Second World War and returned to Liverpool on her last troop voyage in 1948. Canadian Pacific lost many ships during the war and *Empress of Scotland* was one of only three passenger liners to return to service. After a refit she resumed service in 1950 between Liverpool and Quebec, calling at Greenock. When the St Lawrence River iced up in winter, she cruised to the West Indies and South America. Her masts were shortened in 1952 to pass under Quebec bridge to Montreal. She was laid up in Liverpool in 1957, sold to the Hamburg Atlantic Line and renamed *Hanseatic*. She continued trans-Atlantic service between Cuxhaven and New York from 1958 to 1966, when she caught fire in New York harbour and was towed back to Hamburg for scrap. *Empress of Scotland* and *Queen Mary* were the last of the three-funnel liners. *Valentine's postcard*

Right The big ships were as much a part of the cityscape of Liverpool as its imposing shipping offices and classical public buildings. Liverpool was approached from Seacombe and seaward past a line of ocean liners berthed at the 2,533-foot-long **LIVERPOOL LANDING STAGE**, the largest floating structure in the world. Not only liners but also tugs and Irish Sea ferries berthed at Prince's Stage, off Prince's Dock. Here, from the Seacombe ferry steamer in 1950, we see the Bibby Line troopship *Devonshire* and the Elder, Dempster passenger liner *Apapa* together with attendant tugs. The TSMV *Devonshire*, still in wartime grey, was built by Fairfield at Govan (482 feet, 11,275 gross tons) in 1939 as a troopship for the Second World War. Liverpool was the home port for troopships to British overseas posts until 1958. Sea trooping then continued from Southampton for only four years till the end of National Service in 1962, when *Devonshire* was sold to the British India Steam Navigation Company and renamed *Devonia*. She was broken up in 1968. The TSMV *Apapa* was built by Vickers, Armstrong at Barrow in 1947-48 (11,607 gross tons) for Elder, Dempster's West African service. She had a grey hull with a green bottom, white superstructure and a plain buff funnel. She plied from Liverpool to West Africa till 1968, when she was sold to Hong Kong to trade as *Taipooshan*. She was scrapped in 1975. Her younger sister ship *Aureol* was the last passenger liner to leave Liverpool on scheduled service, in 1972.

Below Liverpool landing stage was the departure and arrival point for millions of people: emigrants, statesmen, stars of stage and screen – in fact, anyone travelling between Britain and North America and the far places of the world until ocean liners were eclipsed by jet aircraft travel in the 1960s. When large trans-Atlantic liners were alongside, passenger bridges spanned the stage from its upper deck to the lower passenger decks of the liners, and inclined gangways went down from the ship on to the main deck of the stage for mails, stores and services.

Canadian Pacific's third *Empress of Britain* (640 feet, 25,515 gross tons) was new from Fairfield's yard at Govan in 1956, when she made her maiden voyage from Liverpool on the Montreal run. She is seen here in that year berthed at the landing stage together with two Alexandra tugs astern and an Isle of Man steamer forward. A small Wallasey diesel ferry is arriving at the south end of the stage. The twin-screw turbine steamer *Empress of Britain* was the company's first post-war tonnage and, unlike the pre-war 'Empresses', she had only one funnel, reduced 1st Class cabins for 150 and increased Tourist Class cabins for 900. She began winter cruises to the West Indies from New York in 1960 and from Liverpool in 1962. From 1957 more people were travelling across the Atlantic by air than by sea, and by 1963, only seven years after her maiden voyage, she was withdrawn from the Liverpool-Montreal service and chartered for cruising. She was sold in 1964 to the Greek Line at Piraeus, renamed *Queen Anna Maria* and resumed trans-Atlantic service for ten years, plying between the Mediterranean, Lisbon and New York and cruising in winter. From 1975 she was sold to a succession of cruise lines, being re-named, in turn, *Carnivale*, *Fiesta Marina*, *Olympic* and *Topaz*. Still named *Topaz* and owned by Paradise Cruises of Limassol, she has been on charter to Peace Boat, of Yokohama, since 2003. Refitted in 1965 and 1998, she continues to ply right round the globe every few months promoting international piece, sustainable development and respect for the environment. *Valentine's postcard*

Below In this matching view 45 years earlier in 1911, the famous Cunard liner *Lusitania* is berthed at the stage with the Alexandra tug *Alexandra* astern. The Cunarder was built at John Brown's yard, Clydebank, in 1906-07. She was 790 feet long and almost 31,550 gross tons, and the Mersey at Prince's Stage was specially dredged for her and her sister ship, *Mauretania*, which followed a few months later from the Tyne. The tall funnels that were characteristic of steamships of that period induced a good draught in the boilers.

This four-screw turbine steamer *Lusitania* made her maiden voyage from Liverpool to New York in 1907, and was the first liner to make the Atlantic crossing in less than five days, wresting the coveted Blue Riband of the Atlantic from Germany on her second crossing from Liverpool to New York in 4 days, 19 hours, 52 minutes at an average speed of 24 knots. Her sister, *Mauretania*, took the baton of the Blue Riband in 1909. At the outbreak of the First World War, *Mauretania* was converted to a troopship while *Lusitania* continued in merchant

service. In 1915 'Lucy' was inbound from New York when she was torpedoed by a German submarine and sank off the Old Head of Kinsale, County Cork, with the loss of 1,198 passengers, mostly Americans from what was until then a neutral country. *Mauretania* continued to hold the Blue Riband for an amazing 20 years. From 1929 it passed back to Germany then, in turn, to Italy and France, but Cunard won it back with *Queen Mary* in 1936. The prize passed finally to the United States liner *United States* in 1952. *Valentine's postcard, the late Jack Barlow collection*

Bottom This closer view at a more oblique angle with no liners shows some detail of the Liverpool landing stage, which doubled as Liverpool's promenade. The stage was 2,533 feet (roughly half a mile) long and 80 feet wide, the largest floating structure in the world till it was dismantled in 1973. It floated on 200 iron pontoons and was secured to the river wall by giant mooring chains and by hinged passenger bridges, booms and a floating road, also on pontoons. These allowed the stage to rise and fall with the 31-foot tidal range in the Mersey, giving a low view of the rock-faced, sandstone river wall at low water and a slightly elevated view of the Pier Head at high spring tide. This is a view of the northern end, Prince's Landing Stage, with berths for the Manx and Irish ferries, large ocean liners and tugs. Prince's Stage, off Prince's Dock pier, was built in Wallasey Dock in 1895-96 and joined the north end of George's Landing Stage, off George's Dock pier (now the Pier Head), for the Mersey ferries, to make one long floating structure. The joint was made just north of the 550-foot floating road that served the goods ferries still 1947.

The floating road was still, in the 1950s, used by mail vans and supply and service vehicles to ships at Prince's Stage, and vehicles hoisted aboard the Manx ferries. Prince's Stage was a two-storey, double-deck stage with long ranges of timber buildings housing passenger waiting rooms, refreshment rooms, post, telegraph and telephone offices and customs examining rooms. Berthed at the stage in this 1949 picture are a floating fender (for large liners), a steam tug and a Manx ferry steamer. In the background a Wallasey ferry steamer is swinging into its berth at George's Stage. *Valentine's postcard*

Right In 1964 we are looking down on the working end of two **LIVERPOOL TUGS**, the Alexandra steam tugs *North Light* of 1956 (left) and *Crosby* of 1937, triple-berthed at Prince's Landing Stage. The Alexandra Towing Company was founded at Liverpool in 1887, and its buff, white and black funnelled tugs were also to be found at Southampton and Swansea.

Below Heads are turned as passengers on the foredeck of a Wallasey ferry steamer from Seacombe get this grandstand view of shipping and shipping offices on **LIVERPOOL WATERFRONT**. Now past the liners, we see the Isle of Man Steam Packet berthed at the south end of Prince's Stage loading for Douglas, and a 'Cock' tug of the Liverpool Screw Towage & Lighterage Company at the north end of George's Stage. The bows of the two vessels mark the bottom of the floating road to the landing stage, the point at which Prince's Stage for seagoing ships was joined on to George's Stage for river ferries. At the top of the floating road stands the soot-black lantern steeple of Liverpool's parish church of St Nicholas. The Royal Liver Building, with its twin clock towers, dominates the Mersey scene, more bold in its black suit of soot. Beside it squats the Cunard Building. The offices of 21 shipping lines were housed in these two buildings alone. Our ferry steamer is approaching its berth at George's Landing Stage, springing from the pier that once enclosed the former George's Dock – George's Stage was the original section of the landing stage. The first ferry stage was built in 1847 and was replaced by this one in 1874/6, then Prince's Stage was added in 1896. We can see the glazed, arched porticos to two of the three passenger bridges that sloped up to the tram terminus on George's Pier Head. *Tokim postcard*

Below right A sailing bill of the Liverpool & North Wales Steamship Company for the 1950 season. The Llandudno excursion steamers TSS *St Tudno* of 1926 and TSS *St Seiriol* of 1931 berthed at the landing stage between the Douglas and New Brighton ferries. Steamers had plied between Liverpool and Menai Strait since 1822, landings were made at Llandudno from 1861, and this company was formed in 1891. The company closed down at the end of the 1962 season, but the Liverpool-Llandudno summer sailings were continued by the Isle of Man Steam Packet Company from 1963 to 1980.

Below On the wide, windswept open space of the **PIER HEAD, LIVERPOOL**, between the river wall and the trinity of waterfront buildings, the trams and buses of Liverpool converged on this busy terminus with a grandstand view of the comings and goings of the Mersey ferries and the world's shipping. Wallasey is in the background, a cargo ship and a tug steam up-river and a Wallasey ferry steamer and a Manx ship are berthed at the landing stage. Ferry passengers trooped up the sloping bridges from the landing stage straight on to the tramcars lined up along the top of the river wall on loop lines encircling tram-only roundabouts. On the south island, nearest the camera, the trams circumnavigated a statue of King Edward VII on a horse, erected in 1921. The buses were relegated to the back of the Pier Head, along the front of the Cunard Building and the Dock Building, from which this picture was taken. All the trams and buses are clad in

green, although some of the tramcars are still matt black with soot from years of wartime neglect. The buses in the foreground belong to Crosville Motor Services, of Chester, on routes serving the southern tip of Lancashire between Liverpool and Warrington. The last two buses in the line are of Liverpool Corporation, as are those around the north loop after the closure of the tramlines to the north of the city. A small crowd of people has gathered around a derailed tramcar on the points as it leaves the south loop on route 8 to Garston.

Commercial postcard

Right **PIER HEAD TRAM TERMINUS** was the focal point of the city's 98-mile tramway network. Although there were other city centre tram terminals in Castle Street, Old Haymarket and Lime Street, most tramcars entering the city bore the destination 'PIER HEAD'. There was a constant, stop-start movement of tramcars around the three loop lines with skyward trolleypoles sparking under the cobweb of overhead electric wires, suspended from the lamp posts, as the cars arrived, loaded and departed. Over the sandstone rock garden on the right, fronted by a line of elegant bench seats, four tramcars are lined up around the south loop on routes south to Toxteth, Dingle, Aigburth, Penny Lane and Garston. To the left of this 1950 view we see tramcars on the centre and north loops on routes east and north of the city. George's Pier Head was once the pier that walled off George's Dock from the Mersey when the horse-drawn trams and early electric cars arrived over swing bridges spanning

the dock entrances from the adjoining docks to the south and
north. The dock, dating from 1771, was filled in about 1900 to
provide the sites of the Liver, Cunard and Dock Buildings, built
between 1903 and 1916. The Royal Liver Building, erected in
1908-11, was one of the world's first reinforced concrete, multi-
storey buildings, clad in stone, designed by Aubrey Thomas in
the free commercial style of the period with strong vertical
lines, wide arches, masses of windows and some Art Nouveau
influence. Its fore and aft lantern clock towers are 295 feet tall
with 25-foot-diameter clock dials, the largest in England.

Right Beneath the towering Liver Building and the web of electric
wires, passengers board two Liverpool Corporation tramcars on
the centre loop of the Pier Head terminus in 1954. By this time
the north and south loops had closed, usurped by motorbuses, and
cars on route 19 to Kirkby were loading on the centre loop for lines
east of the city. Kirkby is an industrial estate and satellite new
town on the north-east outskirts of Liverpool and the tramway
system was extended there as late as 1943-44 to serve munitions
and other factories. From Pier Head, trams on route 6A went
alternately via Dale Street and William Brown Street and via
Church Street and Lime Street. The route continued via London
Road, Edge Lane and Broad Green to Bowring Park – 5 miles for
7d in 1957, the last year of the trams. The car on the right is one
of 161 bogie cars built in 1936-37, which proud Liverpolitans
called 'Green Goddesses' or 'Liners'; they were retired from service
in 1955-56. The car on the left is one of 100 shorter, four-wheel
versions nicknamed 'Baby Grands', built in 1937-42; these were
the last tramcars to run in the city.

Below Portrait of nobility: a 'Baby Grand' tramcar poses on the centre loop at **PIER HEAD TRAM TERMINUS** in 1957, against the backdrop of the magnificent classical building of the Mersey Docks & Harbour Board. Built between 1903 and 1907 and clad in white Portland stone, with its great central dome 230 feet high and corner towers with their cupolas, the Dock Building looks like an incongruous mirage of an Indian palace from the ferry approaching Liverpool waterfront. Inside, the spacious marble hall below the dome is awesome. The building formed a splendid backdrop for the equally graceful electric cars that moved about the Pier Head tramway terminus on the riverside. Liverpool tramways closed line by line over a period of nine years from 1948, and tramcars ceased to grace Pier Head and the city streets on 14 September, 1957. The centre loop, for lines east, was the last tramway loop in use, and here, with only a month to go to the end, are two 'Baby Grand' four-wheelers on the last two surviving routes in 1957: the 6A to Bowring Park and the 40 to Page Moss. The front car is No 289, built in 1939. The top-deck passengers and those coming off the trams are enjoying the view of the moving river scene. After the end of the tramways you could still ride Liverpool trams in Glasgow: 46 of the famous 'Green Goddess' bogie cars were sold to the city in 1953-54 and continued in service on Clydeside until 1960, two years before the closure of the Glasgow system.

Bottom Bowling along the front of the buildings on Pier Head, 'Green Goddess' bogie car 964, of 1937, leaves the riverside terminus beneath the vast span of overhead rigging and sets out on its 9-mile odyssey to Everton, Walton, Gillmoss and Kirkby. Its journey will take it through the city centre via Church Street and Lime Street. It will scale the heights of Everton on one-way single lines through the former village streets, pass Everton football ground and speed along reserved tracks that stretch 4½ miles along Walton Hall Avenue and East Lancashire Road. In its 98 miles of tramways, Liverpool had 28 miles of reserved tracks alongside roads or in the median strips of dual carriageways, constructed from 1914 to 1944 but not

used by the replacement buses. Route 19 saw the last extension of the reserved tracks, at Kirkby in 1944, but the line closed in 1956, to be replaced by buses on the roads. On the right a 1949 Crossley-bodied Crossley bus is loading for Speke. The rusticated facade of the Cunard Building (1914-16) stands on the extreme right, next to the Liver Building, and the equestrian statue of King Edward VII is silhouetted against the superstructure and funnel of the Cunard liner *Saxonia*, about to sail on its maiden voyage in 1954.

Above The Liver Building is on our left and the Cunard Building on our right as we head up **WATER STREET** into the city from the waterfront in 1954. The Liverpool Overhead Railway (LOR) spans the street behind the buildings and the street rises to the classical portico of the Town Hall, which juts out in soot-black silhouette at the top of the street. Beyond the Town Hall we see the black steeple of the Municipal Buildings in Dale Street. Water Street and Dale Street were the main axis of the city, leading in a straight line from the waterfront to London Road. A Liverpool Corporation bus, a Weymann-bodied Leyland Titan PD2 of 1952, stands at the corner of the Liver Building, poised for a run on route 79 to Childwall and Belle Vale.

Right Underneath the Overhead: crossing two railways at once, a Corporation bus and tramcar hammer over the dock railway tracks as they duck under the LOR on their way along the last reach of **WATER STREET** to the Pier Head in 1954. Sometimes they had to stop and wait for a goods train ambling along the dock railway behind a man walking with a red flag. The main line of

the Mersey Docks & Harbour Board railway ran for most its 6 miles from Dingle to Bootle beneath the colonnade of the Overhead Railway, nicknamed the 'dockers' umbrella', alongside the dock road (right) to all dockyard gates and the ramifications of an 81-mile railway system around the docks. This section, behind the Pier Head buildings, linking the older southern docks with the newer northern docks, closed in 1971. This stretch of the dock road is still called George's Dock Gate; the old nameplate on the churchyard wall is now the only memorial to the dock here that was filled in to provide the site of the Liver, Cunard and Dock Buildings. The soot-black church steeple on the extreme right, built in 1815, survived the bombing of the 18th-century nave of the old parish church of St Nicholas in 1940, and the church was rebuilt in stone to match the tower in 1949-52. Between the church and the warehouse beyond is the dock road entrance to the Mersey Tunnel. Above it, the large circular advertisement on the end of the warehouse is for Henry Diaper & Co, warehouse-owners, shippers and forwarding agents, of King Edward Street.

This page At **PIER HEAD STATION** one could climb the stairs and board a train to Canada. Veteran, brown, teak electric trains rumbled over an iron and steel colonnade 16 feet above the dock road and paused in this elevated wooden station behind the Liver Building. The LOR was the first electric elevated railway in the world when it opened in 1893 from Herculaneum Dock to Alexandra Dock with 500V dc third rails. The line was extended north to Seaforth Sands in 1894, south – in tunnel – to Dingle in 1896, and north again in 1905 to Seaforth & Litherland, a junction with the Lancashire & Yorkshire Railway's electric line from Liverpool Exchange to Southport. The original electric trains of 1893-99, one of which is seen in the station, ran to the end in 1956, but seven of the 19 three-car sets were rebodied in 1947-55. There were 17 stations in 7 miles, 12 of them named after the docks they served (without the suffix 'Dock'), so trains called at Herculaneum, Toxteth, Brunswick, Wapping, Canning, Clarence, Nelson, Huskisson, Canada, Brocklebank, Alexandra and Gladstone. The railway carried dockers, seamen and shipping clerks to and from work and attracted sightseers to sample an elevated view of ships in dock, otherwise hidden behind high walls. John Betjeman wrote in 1955 that the Overhead was the 'best way of imbibing a quick general impression of Liverpool's atmosphere, architecture and activity in a short time'. For a brief period, from 1905 to 1913, L&YR electric trains ran along the Overhead from Southport to

Dingle via the junction at Litherland. From 1906 LOR trains ran over an L&YR goods line to Aintree on race days.

The American motorcar sweeping past the station in this 1954 picture was the Canadian Pacific staff car from the Liver Building: a dark blue 1952 Chevrolet; Canadian Pacific moved its British office from London to the Liver Building in 1948. The Liverpool Corporation bus is a 1954 Crossley-bodied AEC on route 79 to Belle Vale. The Overhead girders were constantly repainted, like the Forth Bridge, but salt and soot corrosion took its toll and neither the company nor the Corporation could afford to rebuild the railway. The last trains ran at the end of 1956, the demolition men moved in and by 1959 an integral feature of Liverpool had disappeared.

Above right With the Royal Liver Building looming in the background and the Overhead Railway spanning the street, a Corporation tramcar crests the slope of **WATER STREET** and swings into the curve around the front of the Town Hall on route 44 to Gillmoss. The head office of Martin's Bank is on the right and the India Building on the left, both steel-framed, eight-storey buildings clad in Portland stone, designed by Herbert Rowse in the 1920s in his North American classical skyscraper style. The India Building was badly damaged in the 1941 blitz and the architect supervised its restoration. Both buildings house a multitude of financial, shipping and other commercial offices; in 1955 tenants of the India Building included

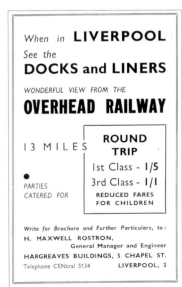

Wallasey Embankment Commissioners, Clyde Shipping Company, Liverpool Screw Towing & Lighterage Company, Manchester Lines, Manchester Ship Canal Company, the Passport Office, Blue Funnel Line and Elder, Dempster Lines. The building fills the entire block between Fenwick Street and Drury Lane and is traversed by a barrel-vaulted arcade of shops from Water Street to Brunswick Street. It also houses an entrance to a pedestrian subway leading under two blocks from Water Street to James Street station on the Mersey Railway. Streamlined tramcar 227, a four-wheel 'Baby Grand' built in 1938, is bound along Scotland Road, Walton Lane and East Lancashire Road. The 44 was the last tram route along Scotland Road when it closed in 1956. *Author's collection*

Right The view down Water Street was the dramatic last reach of the main road through the city to the waterfront. In this 1963 photograph the black bulk of the Liver Building towers overall, its fore and aft clock towers topped by 18-foot effigies of the mythical Liver Bird (resembling a cormorant). After 1957 Liverpool seemed strangely empty without its tram tracks and overhead wires and the constant hum, ring and hiss of the ubiquitous electric cars, although the tracks can still be seen in situ at the lower end of Water Street between the Liver and Cunard Buildings six years after abandonment. The building beyond the lantern and rusticated stonework of the Town Hall is the head office of Martin's Bank, founded in 1831 as the Bank of Liverpool. This eight-storey building was erected in 1927-32 and housed general offices on the seven floors above the bank, including the French Consulate, United Molasses and Bibby Line. The building was designed by Herbert Rowse, architect of the Mersey Tunnel entrances and ventilation shafts, with similar classical and Art Deco features. He made his office on the top floor. Other buildings in the street were financial and shipping offices.

Below Sunday morning is the time to take stock of Liverpool's commercial and civic architecture. Here in 1963 the classical profile of the **TOWN HALL** projects halfway across the top of Water Street and the line of Dale Street beyond at the junction with Castle Street (left) in the commercial heart of Liverpool. The Town Hall was built in 1748-54 in the Palladian style by John Wood the younger of Bath. After a fire in 1795 it was remodelled and enlarged by James Wyatt of London over a period to 1820; he added the lantern dome and the Corinthian portico. The council offices moved to the Municipal Buildings in Dale Street in 1866. The interior of the Town Hall is impressive: the grand stairway under the lantern dome, the panelled council chamber and the palatial ballroom and banqueting room, the small ballroom and the three reception rooms, all described by King Edward VII as the finest suite of rooms in England. A bomb damaged the council chamber and shattered the windows during the May 1941 blitz. The building on the left is the head office of Martin's Bank (1927-32, formerly the Bank of Liverpool). On the right is the District Bank (formerly the Manchester & Liverpool District Bank) on the facing corner of Lower Castle Street, the Midland Bank (formerly the London City & Midland Bank) on the facing corner of Castle Street and, beyond it, the golden lantern cupolas of Francis Doyle's Royal Insurance Building.

Bottom The Town Hall, at the apex of the junction with Water Street (left) and Dale Street (right), dramatically terminates the vista along Castle Street, a red-asphalted carriageway suitably flanked by handsome 19th-century office buildings. It stands slightly off-centre because Castle Street was widened on one side only in the 1820s. The bold

Italian Doric front of the Liverpool Branch of the Bank of England, built in 1845-48, marks the corner of Cook Street (right); this was one of three provincial branches designed by Charles Cockerell. Next to it are the classical columnar facades of the Norwich Union Insurance Society and Barclay's Bank. The offices of accountants, building societies and insurance companies continue to the corner of Dale Street, with shops on the street, among them notably Charles Wilson's bookshop and Austin Reed, the tailor. The turreted building on the left is the Overseas Branch of the Midland Bank on the corner of Brunswick Street, which leads down to the Pier Head, emerging between the Cunard and Dock Buildings. In 1963 a green Liverpool Corporation bus, a 1962 Metropolitan Cammell-bodied Leyland Atlantean, advances along route 79C from Pier Head to Wavertree and Lee Park. This front-entrance, rear-engine design, still standard today, was pioneered by Wallasey Corporation in 1958 and was in general use by the late 1960s.

Below The dome of the Victoria Monument (left) complements the dome of the Town Hall at the end of **CASTLE STREET** (right). Before the war the Customs House at the opposite end of South Castle Street mirrored the Town Hall in its architecture and blackness, and the three domes could be seen in one length of street. Castle Street was the main street of the fortified medieval town, and the 13th-century castle, on the south wall of the fortification, stood on the site of the Victoria Monument. The castle fell into disuse after the Civil War of 1642-45 and was demolished in 1709-20 to be

replaced by St George's Church and a market place. The Georgian-style church was one of ten parish churches built by Liverpool Corporation in the 18th century for the growing population of the city and was the fashionable church patronised by the City Council. As part of its street-widening programme, the Corporation cleared the slum houses of Castle Ditch in 1827 and built the handsome St George's Crescent of Regency houses and shops flanking the entrance of Lord Street, alas destroyed in the Second World War. The church closed in 1902 with the depopulation of the commercial city centre, leaving the site vacant for a memorial to Queen Victoria. The 14-foot bronze statue was erected in 1904 under a dome on clustered Ionic columns on a stepped and balustraded plinth in Portland stone.

The road space around the monument is divided nominally into three segments, with St George's Crescent in the foreground. As in Sydney at the other end of the Empire, the statue of the Empress of Britain was encircled by a tramway loop: this was Castle Street tram terminus. In 1954 a 'Baby Grand' tramcar on route 6A from Bowring Park lumbers over the junction into Derby Square, backed by the Midland Bank, before diving down James Street to Pier Head. The bank was built in 1868 as the head office of the Bank of North Wales. A street running left of the monument, Preeson's Row, formed the third side of this triangular open space. Two Corporation buses turn from Lord Street into Castle Street. The two private cars parked at the foot of the monument are a post-war Ford Popular and a 1952 Sunbeam Talbot coupé.

Above The noble canyon of **DALE STREET** is seen here in 1950 from the Town Hall on the corner of High Street (left). We can see the towers of three of Liverpool's finest buildings on the right-hand side of the street: Francis Doyle's Royal Insurance office (1897-1903) with its golden, lantern cupolas crowning a turreted, Portland stone building on the corner of North John Street; Alfred Waterhouse's Prudential Assurance office (1885-86), vertical Gothic in glazed red brick and terracotta; and the Municipal Buildings (1860-66), soot-black classical with a 200-foot clock tower and French convex roofs. The building on the left, No 1 Dale Street, fronting the block between High Street and Exchange Street, was the office that Charles Cockerell and his son Frederick built in 1855-57 for the Liverpool & London & Globe Insurance Company, founded in Liverpool in 1836. On the next corner, of Exchange Street, were the offices of the Canada Life Assurance Company and the Western Assurance Company, with Tetley's tobacconist shop on the street. The clock on the right marks Pennington & Rigby's jewellery shop, the first of the row of shops on the street frontage of the grimy, columnar Queen Insurance Buildings (1837-39), housing the offices of stockbrokers, accountants, solicitors, insurers, shipping agents and estate agents. Next to the jewellery shop is the entrance to Queen's Arcade. The street is crowded with people, parked cars and slow-moving lines of cars, trams and buses. A streamlined tramcar heads the line of oncoming vehicles on route 29 from Lower Lane, bound for Castle Street terminus; route 29 closed in 1954. *J. Salmon postcard, © The Salmon Picture Library*

Left **LIVERPOOL EXCHANGE STATION**, the former Lancashire & Yorkshire Railway terminus, fronted on to Tithebarn Street and terminated the view up Moorfields. The railway reached this terminus in 1850, then called Tithebarn Street station. It was renamed when it was rebuilt in 1884-86 with a hotel fronting Tithebarn Street, and the facade was designed in a free neo-classical style with columns between the windows. The main station entrance, seen here in 1970, was through twin Romanesque arches, which were becoming a feature of late-Victorian architecture. The hotel had 150 bedrooms and a ballroom and was entered under an ornate, colonnaded iron portico spanning the footpath. This was the central elevation of a long facade, within which was a long, wide loop road for cabs and a spacious concourse with many shops on a slope rising to the platforms, above street level, under a four-gabled trainshed.

The L&YR was early in the field of electric railways, electrifying the lines to Southport in 1904 and Ormskirk in 1913 on the third-rail system, with frequent multiple-unit trains. The company became part of the London, Midland & Scottish Railway in 1923, and LMS electric trains, introduced in 1939, lasted till 1978, in the subway era. The station was closed for three months during the Second World War after damage to the trainshed and the viaduct on the approach. Trains left Exchange along a viaduct over north dockland to Southport, Wigan, Preston, Blackpool, Blackburn, Manchester, Rochdale, Todmorden, Bradford, Leeds, Windermere, Carlisle, Newcastle, Glasgow and Edinburgh. The station closed in 1977, the electric trains went underground to Liverpool Central Low Level, and the remaining services were diverted to Lime Street.

Top Viewed here from Dale Street, the **OLD HAYMARKET**, the Mersey Tunnel entrance and St John's Gardens form a wide, open space in the cultural centre of the city. The 500-foot St George's Hall is on the right, the Technical School, Museum and Library are ranged up the slope of William Brown Street on the left, and Wellington's column stands in a further open space in the background. The column in the centre of the picture is a fluted 60-foot black granite shaft marking the main entrance to the road tunnel and matches the one at the Birkenhead tunnel entrance; both are monuments to the tunnel's builders of 1926-34. The tunnel entrance occupies the entire triangle in the foreground between Dale Street (left), Manchester Street (right) and Old Haymarket (middle distance). Statues of King George V and Queen Mary, who opened the tunnel in 1934, are silhouetted against the white stone parapet above the tunnel portal. On the apron below St George's Hall are St John's

Gardens, where office workers lunch on the bench seats and sprawl out on the lawns in this oasis among the busy streets in the very heart of the city. Between the gardens and the tunnel entrance is Old Haymarket, now a three-track tram station and siding used as an additional city centre terminus in peak periods. On the left of the picture, tramcars ply along Dale Street and William Brown Street, the main axis of the system between Pier Head and London Road. First in the line of neo-classical civic buildings on William Brown Street is the Technical School (1902), its rusticated ribs picked out in white pigeon guano against the grimy black stonework. *Photochrom postcard*

Above From the echoing roar and hazy light of the modern **MERSEY TUNNEL**, vehicles emerge into a contrasting scene of gigantic black stone buildings and fluted columns like a set from ancient Greece or Rome, and Art Deco street lamps like something out of fairyland. We have arrived in the centre of Liverpool. Ahead of us is William Brown Street with the City Museum and Library and Wellington's column. *Tokim postcard*

Above In August 1961 office workers and shoppers take their ease and enjoy the sun in **ST JOHN'S GARDENS**, backed by the scowling, grimy, classical facades of the Brown Library & Museum, the Picton Reading Room and the Walker Art Gallery on the left, and St George's Hall, silhouetted on the right. The gardens, opened in 1904 on the site of the former St John's churchyard, are one of the few oases of green in the city centre and contain several bronze or stone statuesque monuments to Liverpool's leading citizens and benefactors. The most prominent sculpture is that of the Valkyrie-like Britannia flanked by a soldier of 1685 and one of the Boer War. This is a monument to the officers and men of the King's Liverpool Regiment who fell in the Afghan campaigns (1878-80), in Burma (1885-87) and in the Boer War (1899-1902). In the background is Wellington's column of 1863.

Above right This 1952 view from Wellington's column down **WILLIAM BROWN STREET** to the Mersey Tunnel entrance shows (from the right) the Corinthian colonnades of the Walker Art Gallery, the Picton Reading Room and the Brown Library & Museum. The north end of St George's Hall (left) casts its shadow across the street, with St John's Gardens beyond. Sir Andrew Walker, brewer and Mayor of Liverpool in 1873, paid for the art gallery, built in 1874-77. It fronts on to the lower end of a street called Islington (formerly Islington Row), which led uphill into the inner city slum belt. (Liverpool has five streets with the names of London districts: Islington, Kensington, Paddington, Wapping and Whitechapel.) Rounding off the bend between Islington and William Brown Street is the domed and colonnaded rotunda of the 'reading room' named after Sir James Picton, chairman of the city's Library, Museums and Arts Committee for 40 years. Built in 1875-79, it houses the city's reference library in a circular hall for 200 readers with an amphitheatre beneath for concerts and lectures. Next to the Picton Reading Room is the lending library and museum, built in 1857-60 and named after its

benefactor, Sir William Brown, then MP for South Lancashire, which included Liverpool. This was the first building to be erected in the street, which also takes his name, after the demolition of the old houses on Shaw's Brow. The Brown Library & Museum was badly bomb-damaged and gutted in the May 1941 blitz and lost most of its collection, although the most valuable museum exhibits had been evacuated. The Steble Fountain in the foreground was erected in 1879 and named after Colonel R. F. Steble, Mayor of Liverpool in 1874, but the fountain was usually dry. A 1768 map of Liverpool marks 28 windmills on the skyline. A tumbledown post mill, dating from 1451, the last of the three King's Mills of Liverpool, stood on the site of the Steble Fountain and was demolished in 1780. *Valentine's postcard*

Right Looking across to **LIME STREET** in 1952, the mid-morning sunshine dramatically backlights the fluted stone column of the Wellington Monument, the colonnaded east front of St George's Hall and part of the north apse with its attached columns. A 14-foot statue of Arthur Wellesley, Duke of Wellington, cast from cannon guns captured at the Battle of Waterloo, stands on the top of the 81-foot column, unveiled in 1863. It stands in a triangular site laid out in 1878 between William Brown Street (behind it), Islington (right foreground) and Commutation Row (left). The broad swath of Lime Street, Liverpool's best-known thoroughfare, stretches beyond the column, with the 500-foot length of St George's Hall, acknowledged to be the finest neo-classical building in the world, along the right-hand side. The colonnaded east front and the windowless attic mark the extent inside the building of the 169-foot-long assembly hall. The pilastered extensions on each side of the main hall front the sombre Victorian assize court and civil court, and the north apse houses a semi-circular concert theatre. There is another theatre across the street, the Empire (left), opened in 1925 with a neo-classical facade in Portland stone. It has an auditorium for 2,381 and in the 1950s

it staged ballet, concerts, drama, musicals, opera, pantomime and variety shows. Beyond it is Alfred Waterhouse's stern, black North Western Hotel (1871) with its French Renaissance turrets and pinnacles fronting Lime Street railway terminus. The entrance to London Road is on the left. Lime Street was formerly Limekiln Lane; the kilns stood on the site of Lime Street station and two windmills stood on the site of St George's Hall in the Liverpool of circa 1800. *Valentine's postcard*

Above The image of Liverpool fades suddenly as we leave the architectural splendour of the city centre and head up **LONDON ROAD**. We hear the ebbing hum of a tramcar on route 6A as it ascends the gradient, hounded closely by a horsebox van and a Morris Minor car. In the misty background is the triangle of Monument Place, where the tramcar will fork right into the inner city slum belt over Edge Hill on its way to Bowring Park. The Odeon cinema (right), on the corner of Pudsey Street, is showing *Return To Paradise*, released in 1953, with Gary Cooper on a South Sea island. From the left are Jerome (photographer), The Lord Warden (public house), Camden Street, Hepworth's (tailor), Alexandré (tailor), Halford's (bicycles), Meeson's (confectioner) and The Clock Inn with a projecting square clock as an inn-sign. *Mason's Alpha series postcard*

Above right This was the view of **LIME STREET** for the man in the street who could not attain the lofty viewpoints of the postcard photographer. His view of St George's Hall (left), the Walker Art Gallery and the Wellington Monument (in the background) was always partly obscured by passing trams, buses and cars. Lime Street was Liverpool's best-known thoroughfare, famed for its main railway terminus, its monumental civic buildings, its grand hotels, its department stores and its bright lights – the animated advertisements, a poor imitation of Piccadilly Circus, that lit up the facades on the curve into St George's Place at the top of St John's Lane. The name of Lime Street was also notorious throughout the world among merchant seamen for its seedy trade in prostitution. The early 1960s produced a new play called *No Trams To Lime Street* by Alun Owen, in which three seamen, returning to Liverpool after many years, could no longer make their pilgrimage to Lime Street by tram. There were still trams to Lime Street when this

picture was taken in about 1955. Streamlined, four-wheel 'Baby Grand' car 271, of 1938, bowls past St George's Place (left) up the slight gradient of Lime Street on route 6A to turn up London Road to Bowring Park. Liverpool's last trams went this way in 1957. On the right a 1953 Vauxhall car has just passed a Liverpool Corporation bus, a 1949 Crossley-bodied Crossley, on special service at a stop outside Lime Street station. *Author's collection*

Right The south portico of St George's Hall, like a Greek temple, rises imperiously on its stone-walled podium above the slope of St John's Lane, and theatrically dominates this view up **ROE STREET**. The tympanum in the pediment above the portico is blank; the exuberant bas-relief sculpture, which was the external crowning glory of the building, was removed in the late 1950s as it was in danger of falling out. The seething mass of white figures in Caen stone stood out against the soot-black stonework of the building, which had been cleaned by the time this picture was taken in 1969 to show up the architecture of this masterpiece to better effect in its true honey colours of Darley Dale stone. Part of the North Western Hotel can be seen in Lime Street behind the hall.

The gap on the left of Roe Street is Queen Square, site of a weekday fruit and vegetable market and a car park on Sunday, when this picture was taken. To the left of the square are the Edwardian-baroque Market Branch of the Midland Bank and a boarded-up public house, the Magic Clock, with decorative timber framing. The building on Roe Street beyond the square is the back of the disused Victoria Hotel, fronting St John's Lane. A crossover in the tram tracks in the shadow of the Royal Court theatre (right) was a city centre peak-period terminus for trams going up Lime Street and London Road to Everton and Townsend Lane (route 14A) or on to Utting Avenue East

(route 14); these routes closed in 1955, yet the tracks are still in situ 14 years later. Behind the camera the abandoned tram tracks curved and dipped down Hood Street and across the valley of the former pool to a long-disused terminus in Great Crosshall Street. Street lights still hang from the span wires attached to fixings on the buildings and the traction pole by the telephone kiosk that once supported the overhead electric wires for the trams.

Above The fading Regency gentility of the Victoria Hotel, with peeling stucco and dirty net curtains, and the dingy, baroque, Art Nouveau building next door, both disued by the time of this 1969 photograph, made contrasting bedfellows with the grandeur of the monumental St George's Hall, St John's Gardens and William Brown Street. This was the view from St

George's Hall across **ST JOHN'S LANE**, down Roe Street to Queen Square. The hotel stood on the corner of St John's Lane (right) and Roe Street (left). The grotesquely ornate, narrow building to the right, No 20 St John's Lane, housed the offices of fruit merchants and button merchants in 1950. As seen in the previous picture, Queen Square was in the gap between the back of the Victoria Hotel and the Market Branch of the Midland Bank (left). This was a once fashionable area that was now going to seed – the other face of Liverpool.

Left Ghosts of Regency and Victorian times haunted the derelict buildings and bombed 'toothgaps', and **QUEEN SQUARE** was no longer the salubrious address it had been in the 1830s or even the 1930s, when these Regency terraces were hotels with the classical doorways that survive here. A fruit and vegetable market flourished daily except Sunday, and on a Sunday in 1963 we can see the shuttered stalls of Dan Wuille & Co Ltd and S. C. Saltmarsh Ltd, which encroached on the former hotels. The square was then entirely enclosed by the premises of fruit importers, salesmen and merchants with the exception of the Market Branch of the Midland Hotel and the Royal Court Hotel. Above the ruined, ornate, iron balcony, the words WOODSBEE HOTEL can just be discerned in the peeling stucco; the former Star & Garter Hotel, a continuation of the Regency terrace, had been bombed in the war, and through the gap we can see part of the south portico of St George's Hall, still grimy black, its ledges spattered with pigeon guano and its empty tympanum covered with wire netting. On weekdays the market stalls spread across the square, leaving an aisle for motor traffic. A single horse-tram line with centre grooves still lay in the granite setts through the middle of Queen Square, curving in from Roe Street and winding through reverse curves into Great Charlotte Street. This 19th-century relic was never part of the electric tramway system and survived disused until the area was redeveloped in the 1970s.

Above **CHURCH STREET** is the main shopping street in Liverpool city centre, with most of the large department stores: from the right are Wynn's (house furnisher), Bon Marché (fashions), Basnett Street, Swears & Wells (furriers), Marks & Spencer (department store), Maison Lyons (café and restaurant), and among the other shops to the corner of Whitechapel were the Kardomah Café, William Henderson's drapery and fashion store and Bunney's household and fancy goods store. There was also the Tatler news cinema, owned by Capital & Provincial News Theatres Ltd, with a continuous hourly programme of newsreels and cartoons. The inter-war block on the left, from Church Alley to Church Lane, housed Montague Burton (tailor), F. W. Woolworth (bazaar) and C&A Modes (ladies' outfitters). The older building on the next block to Paradise Street was Cooper's, the old-time, all-round grocers, greengrocers, butchers, tea dealers, wine and spirit merchants, ironmongers, tobacconists and fancy goods dealers. Cooper's also had a café on the first floor with a view of the trolleypoles of the passing tramcars. The shopping centre continued up the sunlit buildings on the north side of Lord Street in the background (the south side of Lord Street was still a bombed site) with the aft clock tower of the Liver Building on the waterfront just visible over the top of the buildings. The tram tracks in the foreground curve into Parker Street and continue behind the camera up Ranelagh Street. The gap on the left was a bombed site, where a block of shops and offices was felled during the war. This was previously the site of St Peter's Church (1704-1919), which gave its name to Church Street. It was the first of the ten churches built by Liverpool Corporation in the 18th century and became the pro-cathedral. *Photochrom postcard*

Above The motley frontage of the north side of **RANELAGH STREET** (pronounced 'Ranley') has a homely, vernacular appeal after the posh shops in Church Street, just around the bend to the left, and Bold Street (Liverpool's Bond Street), the continuation of Church Street to the right. The photograph is taken from Waterloo Place, the junction of the three streets, looking towards Lime Street. On the right is Liverpool Central station and the subway entrance to the low-level terminus of the underground railway from Birkenhead. Behind the station towers the post-war reconstruction of John Lewis's department store, which was destroyed in the May 1941 blitz. At the top of the street we see the black 'gin palace' of The Vines, on Lime Street, and part of the Adelphi Hotel. Centre stage, a 1938 Austin taxicab waits outside the station entrance. Along that motley frontage from the left are Johnson brothers (cleaners and dyers), A. Hyams & Co (Government surplus outfitter), Elsie Bruce (florist), Milk Cocktail Bars Ltd, the Scotch Wool & Hosiery Stores, Charles & Co (jeweller), the Central

Restaurant & Snack Bar, Cases Street, The Midland public house and the Central Hotel. *Tokim postcard*

Below left Exhaust steam echoes under the trainshed of the dingy, railway-mystic **LIVERPOOL CENTRAL STATION** in 1959, with its soot-stained fanlight over the portal. On the roadway for cabs and mail vans between the main-line arrival platforms 1 and 2 are two Liverpool Corporation buses providing Central station's traditional connection with ships at Liverpool Landing Stage. Platforms 3 and 4 are the main-line departure platforms, and an ex-LMS 2-6-4 tank engine with a matching train of ex-LMS compartment carriages in platform 3 awaits the 'right-away' for all stations to Manchester Central. Platforms 5 and 6 were for local services.

From its opening in 1874 till nationalisation in 1948, Liverpool Central was the terminus and headquarters of the Cheshire Lines Committee, a joint system formed by the Midland, Great Central and Great Northern Railways, bringing their trains across rival LNWR territory from Manchester Central to Chester, Liverpool, St Helens and Southport. From the grouping of railways in 1923 the Cheshire Lines became a joint operation of the LMS and LNER. The railway approached Liverpool Central through the 1,320-yard Great George Street Tunnel on a rising gradient of 1 in 90 and terminated in a confined wedge between Bold Street, Ranelagh Street and Renshaw Street, with only 250 yards from the tunnel mouth to the buffer stops. The main span of the roof over platforms 1 to 5 was 164 feet wide and 65 feet high; a narrow span covered platform 6. Central station was host to a variety of locomotives and rolling-stock from the constituent companies, and even the North Eastern and Great Eastern.

From these platforms you could ride through to Matlock and St Pancras, to Nottingham Victoria and Marylebone, to Sheffield, Hull, Lincoln, Grimsby, Cromer, Great Yarmouth,

Cambridge and Harwich. There were express and stopping services to Warrington Central and Manchester Central and local services on a circuitous belt line to Aintree Central and Southport Lord Street. Downstairs was the dimly-lit Low Level station with an island platform, terminus of the Mersey Railway electric trains to Rock Ferry, New Brighton and West Kirby. The Southport service closed north of Aintree in 1952, most of the other services lasted into the 1960s, and the great station closed in 1972, with only a cut-back suburban service to Gateacre. The underground station was modernised in 1976-77 and is still open.

Above The massive, seven-storey **ADELPHI HOTEL** dominates Ranelagh Place at this six-way street junction on the edge of the city centre. It was built in 1912-13 in a free-style Queen Anne manner for the Midland Railway, one of the three partners in the Cheshire Lines Committee, which had its headquarters at Central station just down Ranelagh Street to the left, and was originally named the Midland Adelphi. It was built with an eye to the trans-Atlantic trade and for this the railway company engaged as its architect Frank Atkinson, who designed the saloons of ocean liners of the period, and this is evident in the style of the stately interior. Next to it is the grotesque black Edwardian-baroque 'gin palace' of The Vines (1907) with its cut-glass windows and richly ornate interior like a banking hall with a skylight dome. The two street lamps on the island in the middle of Ranelagh Place are identical to the Art Deco, half-moon examples at the Mersey Tunnel entrance in Old Haymarket. The black bulk of St George's Hall terminates the distant view along Lime Street. Beyond Lime Street and Ranelagh Place we leave the city centre and climb the ridge of Edge Hill. Copperas Hill runs up between The Vines and the Adelphi. Right of the Adelphi is the entrance to the fork of Brownlow Hill and Mount Pleasant, while Renshaw Street stretches behind the camera. *Tokim postcard*

still lit the driveway, and a 1950s Cadillac automobile completes the classical twilight scene.

Below The streets running inland from Hope Street and the Cathedral are an area of faded late-Georgian, or Regency, gentility with red-brick or stuccoed terraced houses, some in squares around gardens, and occasional neo-Greek buildings in stone or stucco. Most of the area was built after the end of the Regency period but this style of architecture was still in vogue. **CANNING STREET**, built in the 1830s, is the central axis of this area and we are looking west from Falkner Square to the Cathedral in 1971.

There are shades of Regency Cheltenham in the stuccoed terrace of houses on the north side of **FALKNER SQUARE**, laid out in 1835 as a private square around central, communal gardens. Residents of the square included the Portuguese consul, the vicar of St Saviour's Church, two doctors and a professional photographer at the time of this 1971 photograph.

Not all the residents of the Regency area enjoyed the same standard of living or the same good neighbours. Many of the houses on the fringe of the area, like these on the east side of Falkner Square, had become the tenements of poorer people with absent landlords and were in a very neglected condition and an advanced state of decay in 1971. Regency stucco weathered badly in the salty, sooty air.

There are secluded Regency villa colonies on the waterfront north and south of the city. Out in the bosky southern suburbs, between Aigburth and Garston, **GRASSENDALE PARK** is a residential park of early Victorian villas, built in the 1840s but still in the Regency style, in a woodland setting sloping down to the Mersey bank 5 miles up-river from Liverpool Pier Head, with its own esplanade looking out across 2 miles of water to the Cheshire bank at Bromborough. This 1978 picture shows the park gate pillars and lodge. The estate has its own railway station, Cressington & Grassendale (1873), well-preserved in a cutting, with glass canopies and a three-storey Gothic station house, on the former Cheshire Lines route to Manchester.

Down in dockland, warehouses surrounded the wedge-shaped **BALTIC FLEET TAVERN** on the corner of Hurst Street (left) and a stretch of the dock road called Wapping (right), seen here in 1977. The tavern was named after a large Finnish fleet of three- and four-masted barques, based in the Åland islands, that still sailed, undermanned and uninsured, in the Australian grain trade in the 1920s and '30s, undercutting steamship tariffs and making fast passages in the old clipper tradition. Several of these barques sailed into the Mersey and berthed at grain wharves on both sides of the river.

The five-storey Wapping Dock warehouse (right), colonnaded on the quayside, was built in 1850-57. It survived a fire in the 1940 blitz and the new brickwork at the south end shows where it was rebuilt. Beyond it in silhouette stand the granaries of the Liverpool Grain Store & Transit Company at Coburg Dock: a brick silo of 1906 (on the left) and a tall concrete one of 1936 (on the right), linked by a high-level, covered footbridge. The dock railway and the Overhead Railway used to run along the river side of the dock road and the warehouses were a sounding board to the drone and rumble of the vintage electric trains overhead. The elevated Wapping station was at the far end of Wapping warehouse. Below it, the dock railway tracks swung across the road into the vast Wapping goods station, built in 1829-30, the dockside terminus of the pioneer Liverpool & Manchester Railway (later the LNWR), reached by tunnel from Edge Hill, 1 mile 580 yards long, on a gradient of 1 in 48. This railhead was the fount from which sprang the dock railway system.

Most of Liverpool's oldest docks lay behind the warehouses along the Wapping section of the dock road: Salthouse Dock (1753), Duke's Dock (1773), King's Dock (1788), Albert Dock (1845), Wapping Basin and Wapping Dock (1858). Barges from the Duke of Bridgewater's Canal (Manchester to Runcorn) floated through twin stone arches to load inside the Duke's Warehouse (1811). The Sentinel Waggon Works, of Shrewsbury, had a service depot on the south side of Duke's Dock for steam lorries, which worked in Liverpool dockland until 1962. Wapping goods station closed in 1965.

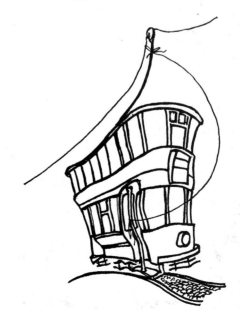

Below A colonnade of massive cast-iron Roman Doric shafts lines the granite quay in the quadrangle of warehouses around **ALBERT DOCK**. Liverpool's Dock Engineer, Jesse Hartley, designed the 7-acre dock in 1839 with five-storey warehouses flush with the quayside for cargoes to be unloaded and hoisted direct into the warehouses to cut the risk of damage and pilferage in transit to inland warehouses. Opened by Prince Albert in 1845, it was the first dock in Liverpool to be enclosed by warehouses. Hartley was Dock Engineer from 1824 to 1860 and in that time he built or rebuilt all docks from Brunswick in the south to Huskisson in the north. His docks were built in an indestructible jigsaw of Scottish granite, flush-faced and curved at the corners. He had fireproof warehouses built entirely of brick and stone on iron framework, with vaulted brick ceilings supporting brick floors above. In its heyday Albert Dock was part of the veritable forest of masts and funnels along the Liverpool waterfront as ships berthed two or three abreast at the wharves. In 1969 Albert Dock is now disused, silent and silting up with river mud, and was among the older, smaller southern docks from Pier Head to Dingle that closed in 1972.

Below In north dockland, warehouses lined most of the streets sloping down to the river between Great Howard Street and the dock road. The warehouses in **BARTON STREET**, seen here in 1974, had canopies over the loading bays and high-level footbridges spanning the street between upper floors. Glasgow Street (first left) and Greenock Street (second left) linked up with Galton Street and Paisley Street to the south. Dundee Street, Neptune Street and Formby Street were the next streets north of Barton Street. These streets were a warren of mills and warehouses with a mixture of pleasant and pungent smells. There was a tannery in Greenock Street and a marine engineering works in Paisley Street. Most of the warehouses in Barton Street belonged to J. Bibby & Sons, seed millers, producing cattle feed, edible oils and soap, with a head office in nearby King Edward Street. Bibby also had premises in Neptune Street and Formby Street and a staff dental clinic in Galton Street. Waterloo Road, a section of the dock road, runs across the bottom of Barton Street, and behind the dockyard wall towers the architectural mass of the six-storey grain warehouses around three sides of Waterloo Dock. They were built in 1867,

each in red brick on rock-faced, granite arcading, with round-headed windows, pilasters and a brick entablature on top, designed by George Lyster, Liverpool's Dock Engineer from 1861 to 1897.

Above Through grim **CHADWICK STREET** in the north of the city, sooty, shabby double-deck tramcars on line 17 from Pier Head to Seaforth swung one block west from Pall Mall to Great Howard Street under the viaducts of the former Lancashire & Yorkshire Railway. The tramline closed at the end of 1950 but the path of the tram tracks remained, marked in this 1964 view by the line of longitudinal granite setts laid after the rails were removed. The tracks passed to

the left of the island with the two gas lamps under the girder bridge carrying trains from Southport, Preston and Wigan into Liverpool Exchange terminus. They then divided to pass beneath the brick arches of the second viaduct carrying the freight branch into Great Howard Street goods station. New brickwork on the parapet of the viaduct is repair of war damage. Through the twin arches over the street we can see part of Waterloo goods station (1849-1963) on the corner of Great Howard Street (crossing) and Oil Street (opposite) running down to the dock road. Waterloo, like Wapping, was another huge LNWR goods station reached by a tunnel from Edge Hill, 2 miles 37 yards long, on a gradient of 1 in 56/60. Boat trains gave posh liner passengers an insight into the real Liverpool as they were routed through this tunnel, the gloomy goods station and the dockyards to get to and from Riverside station.

Above right Underneath the Arches: a Liverpool Corporation tramcar passes under the railway bridges in Chadwick Street inbound on route 17 from Seaforth to Pier Head in 1948. Car

846 was one of 49 Marks Bogie cars built at Edge Lane works in 1935-36 on EMB bogies with Crompton Parkinson motors. They took their name from Walter Marks, the City Transport Manager from 1934 to 1948, who redesigned the internal layout of the new cars from that of the previous batch of 35 Robinson Cabin cars of 1933, which were similar in external appearance, the design of the City Electrical Engineer, Mr P. J. Robinson. Mr Marks extended and modernised the tramway system with several more miles of street track and roadside reservation from 1935 to 1944, and 161 streamlined double-deck cars built in 1936-37. He was also President of the Light Railway Transport League, and in 1945 produced a plan to extend and modernise the system further, switching 32 miles of street track to reservation in widened roads, new lines to outlying housing estates and a fleet of North American-style single-deck cars. The City Council opted for the cheaper conversion to motorbuses, which began in 1948. Route 17 closed in 1950, the Marks Bogie cars disappeared in 1951-55 (car 846 going in 1953), and the last two lines of the system closed in 1957. *Ted Gahan*

Above Cheshire looks at Lancashire: the Mersey (Anglo-Saxon 'Maeres-ea', 'boundary river') is the boundary between Cheshire and Lancashire and was originally part of the Humber-Mersey line that formed the boundary between the midland kingdom of Mercia and the northern kingdom of Northumbria in the Anglo-Saxon heptarchy. In 1954 the smoky north dockland of Liverpool is viewed across the Mersey from the **NORTH MEAD** site of Wallasey Town Hall at Seacombe. The Douglas ferry TSS *Ben My Chree* of the Isle of Man Steam Packet Company rides at anchor in mid-river. The Mersey is the gulf between sylvan Cheshire and industrial Lancashire, symbolised by the birch trees on the grassy cliff top of North Mead and the smokestacks of Clarence Dock Power Station (centre) and Tate & Lyle's sugar refinery (right) at the end of Love Lane. The dark bulk behind the ship is Stanley

Dock tobacco warehouse at the entrance of the Leeds & Liverpool Canal.

The Manx ship *Ben My Chree* was a twin-screw turbine steamer built by Cammell, Laird at Tranmere in 1926-27 (355 by 46 feet, 2,586 gross tons). She was a troopship during the Second World War, based in Scottish ports, and made three trips in the evacuation of Dunkirk. She worked the ferry services from Douglas to Liverpool, Fleetwood, Belfast and Ardrossan and made her last trip, to Liverpool, in 1965 to be laid up in Morpeth Dock, Birkenhead, then towed to Belgium for scrap.

Below The curved brickwork of the dockyard wall, of the north warehouse and of the hydraulic power station with its octagonal, castellated, stone water tower and octagonal brick

chimney, all built for the opening of **STANLEY DOCK** in 1848, display the solid, functional style and craftsmanship that was the hallmark of Jesse Hartley, Liverpool's Dock Engineer from 1824 to 1860. Hartley also introduced railways into the dockyards and hydraulic power to work the dock gates, bridges, capstans and hoists. A dock railway line swung across the road here, disappeared between the massive stone gate towers and passed between the north warehouse and the dockyard wall alongside Walter Street (left), then crossed the street into the L&YR's North Docks goods station. This stretch of the dock road is Regent Road, and the shadow on the right of this 1974 photograph is cast by the massive fortress wall Hartley built the full length of his dockyards to guard

against theft. Stanley Dock is the only dock inland of the dock road, and is the western terminus of the Leeds & Liverpool Canal, which rises above the dock in a flight of five locks. The steel drawbridge here spans the passage between Stanley Dock and Collingwood Dock (to the right), giving access through Salisbury Dock to the river. The Overhead Railway and the main line of the dock railway spanned the waterway on a double-deck swing bridge alongside the road bridge. The last trains along here ran on the Overhead in 1956 and on the dock railway in 1970. Beyond the bridge, on the other side of Stanley Dock, stands that colossus of warehouses, the Stanley Dock Tobacco Warehouse, 730 feet long, 165 feet wide and 125 feet tall, with 36 acres of storage on 14 floors. It was built in 1900 and consumed 6,000 tons of ironwork and 27 million bricks. It is the largest warehouse in Britain.

Top **BOUNDARY STREET** and **LUTON STREET** present a neat, complete townscape of houses, warehouses and public houses, dominated and hemmed in by railways. Viewed from the corner of Great Howard Street in 1964, the scene is framed by an L&YR girder bridge crossing dockland to North Docks goods station on Walter Street, and to high-level coaling staithes on Bramley Moore Dock. The street ends under an arch of the L&YR viaduct to Exchange station, and beyond can be glimpsed the Cheshire Lines' Huskisson goods station. Pigeons are the only form of life in this quiet Sunday morning scene and the headless gas lamp on the left adds to the air of desolation. The street was lined with warehouses on both sides except for the terrace of four houses on the right, complete with their front steps and iron balustrades, and the two dingy corner taverns on the near corners of the two side streets on the right. The Northern Light public house stood in the shade of the railway bridge on the corner of Newport Street (first right) and the George & Dragon was on the next corner, where Boundary Street turns right, following the old northern boundary of the city of Liverpool. Luton Street runs from the corner of Boundary Street to the railway arch with warehouses all the way.

Above These modest Regency terraced houses, built in 1825, line the waterfront along **MARINE CRESCENT** and Marine Terrace, Waterloo, 5 miles down-river from Liverpool Pier Head, and look out across Liverpool Bay along the Wirral coast to north Wales. They were photographed in 1978.

Storm clouds gather over **LIVERPOOL'S NORTHERN DOCKS** and a freighter rides at anchor on the river with attendant tugs waiting for high water to pass through the dock entrance locks. The superstructure of a Canadian Pacific 'Empress' liner in dock peers over the river wall and dockyard cranes reach skyward along the horizon. The northern docks from Sandon (1851) to Gladstone (1928) were Liverpool's newer and larger docks, where business concentrated as ships grew larger. They are the outer end of the 7-mile line of docks along the Liverpool waterfront to Bootle at the mouth of the river, and are still in use today. They extend up to 660 yards from the dock road into the river, having been built along the broad sands of Liverpool's north shore, which was previously described as the finest stretch of bathing beach in Lancashire. Early-19th-century paintings show bathing-machines, sand dunes, cottages and windmills along the shore from Liverpool to the former village of Bootle, an idyllic, rural scene that was reflected in the incongruous names of Sandhills and Seaforth Sands railway stations in dockland. We are looking at the stretch of dock wall enclosing Langton and Alexandra Docks in Bootle. The dock wall, ships and cranes were the incongruous backdrop of the view east across the river from the seaside holiday resort of New Brighton, although the holidaymakers could also look north out to sea. The picture was taken from a Wallasey ferry approaching New Brighton Pier in 1964.

THE HINTERLAND

The wooded ridge that formed the backdrop of Birkenhead could be seen from almost every street in town, from Wallasey across the docks and from Liverpool across the river. Its bosky outline was a constant reminder that the countryside was not far away because the ridge was a watershed between town and country. Over the hill we were out in rural Wirral and, from the other side, the ridge hid Birkenhead and the whole of industrial Merseyside from that placid, rural idyll, except where the inter-war semi-detached houses along Woodchurch Road spilled over the ridge at Prenton. From the lanes and field paths around Landican and Noctorum you would never have suspected that Merseyside was just over the hill and that Woodside Ferry was only 3 miles away. Nor would you have suspected that you were still, nominally, in Birkenhead, but most of the country we are looking at in this part was the rural hinterland within the County Boroughs of Birkenhead and Wallasey, from Landican to Leasowe.

We have traversed the streets from New Ferry to New Brighton, 6 miles in a straight line from south to north, but now we are glad to leave the bricks and the smoke and the crowds behind us and relax in the embrace of Mother Nature. If we travelled from east to west, only 2¼ miles from the town centre of Birkenhead on the road to Upton we were up in the country and fresh air on Flaybrick Hill, 175 feet above the Mersey. Only 3 miles from Woodside Ferry along the Hoylake road and a quarter of a mile from the end of town the road wound its way through the small, rustic, Christmas-card village of Bidston with its 16th-, 17th- and 18th-century church tower, houses and barns, all in red sandstone, nestling below the northern slopes of Bidston Hill at the north end of the ridge.

Roads climb Bidston Hill through cuttings in the red rock, topped by silver birches and pines, and you can walk up narrow, sandy paths between ferns and rhododendrons to the heathery summit plateau, paved by nature with weather-smoothed slabs of red sandstone. Bidston Mill, humble ancestor of Birkenhead's great flour-milling industry, is a stout, stone tower windmill of 1791, standing on the highest point of the summit plateau, 238 feet high. The mill is owned and preserved by the borough council and its sky-reaching sail frames, which ceased turning in 1864, are a landmark from most points of the compass. On the northern edge of Bidston Hill, overlooking the sea, are a disused lighthouse and the rock-faced Liverpool Observatory & Tidal Institute, with its twin white telescope domes. The observatory (now also disused) gave us the tide tables for the British Isles and two-thirds of the world, issued shipping forecasts and set ships' chronometers.

From the top of Bidston Hill we looked east over the dark gulf of the Mersey in which chimney stacks, cranes, derricks, masts and funnels stood out in the smoky haze. Beyond was the unmistakable black bulk of the lordly Liver Building fronting the great city of Liverpool. We looked north over Bidston Moss with its railway marshalling yards, clattering electric trains and golf links to Wallasey, snug and majestic on its church-crowned plateau. We looked north-west to the spreading suburban sprawl of Leasowe and Moreton, backed by the sandhills along the north Wirral coast. Beyond, the blue Irish Sea shimmered and scintillated in the sunlight and a Manx or Irish ferry was steaming into Liverpool Bay. And we looked west over the successive wooded ridges of Wirral, backed by the dim, grey outline of the hills and mountains of Wales. On top of Bidston Hill we were right on the edge, looking into two different worlds.

Among the pinewoods and rhododendrons below the open hilltop nestle late-Victorian, Ruabon-brick and timber-framed villas, built by Liverpool ship-owners and cotton merchants in spacious grounds, hardly visible among the high hedges and tall trees except for the odd tall chimney or timbered gable peering above the foliage. South of Upton Road, separated from Claughton by the Wirral Golf Course and entirely hidden within a hushed wood, is Noctorum, a secluded, almost dreamworld colony of awesome large houses, shaded by the tall birches, larches and pines. This most exclusive suburb of Birkenhead was home to 192 residents in the 1951 census.

Emerging into the sunlight on the other side of Noctorum wood, South Road was a broad cart-track along the west side of the ridge, and my favourite cycle path into the country, giving a wide view across the cornfields and coverts of the vale of mid-Wirral.

THE WIRRAL PENINSULA

This rectangular, western horn of Cheshire was known as the Hundred of Wirral for more than 900 years. The Saxon Kings of Wessex divided the counties into hundreds, nominally areas of 100 hides of land or their equivalent product in taxes. The hundred was a unit of local government that was extended to the midland shires of Mercia in the early 11th century to consolidate Saxon rule 100 years after the Norse settlement of Wirral. The hundred moot was an open-air assembly at Willaston, rather like the Norse assembly at Thingwall, which it eclipsed. It was a court responsible for collecting taxes, raising armies, arresting offenders, settling disputes and rounding up stray cattle. The assembly met every four weeks throughout nine centuries. With the development of a more sophisticated judicial system, the hundred court declined to a local civil and debtors' court in Neston, then the largest town in Wirral, and was wound up in 1816.

The Wirral peninsula, just 18 miles long from the Vale of Broxton to the sea and 6 to 8 miles across its girth between the wide estuaries of the Mersey and the Dee, was a very precious stretch of country to the townspeople of Birkenhead and Wallasey. They never tired of exploring its field paths and byways on foot and on two wheels, armed with their canvas-covered guide books and canvas-backed maps.

A philanthropic Birkenhead Corporation bought 50 acres of rock and heather on Thurstaston Hill (300 feet), overlooking the Dee estuary, in 1881, 90 acres of Bidston Hill between 1894 and 1908, and the 425-acre grounds of Arrowe Hall, now Arrowe Park, at Woodchurch, in 1927. The Corporation bought these open spaces when they lay outside the borough to save them from builders and keep them for public recreation and nature reserves. Bidston, Prenton and Thingwall were annexed to the borough in 1928 and the boundary was ultimately extended to Noctorum, Upton and Arrowe Park in 1933. Thurstaston still lay 1½ miles

west of the borough boundary but, after the 1881 purchase, one could say that the top of Thurstaston Hill, the scenic high point of Wirral, was in the borough of Birkenhead.

Birkenhead Corporation buses also ran country services well beyond the borough boundary, and in 1950 published the guide book *By Bus Through The Wirral*. It was unusual in those days of regulation for municipal trams or buses to run beyond the borough boundary, but Birkenhead Corporation was already running into the neighbouring boroughs of Bebington and Wallasey when, in 1930, it made a through-running agreement with the country bus company, Crosville, of Chester. Until then, passengers to or from Chester, Neston and West Kirby had to change at the Corporation tram terminals. Now Crosville buses could run through to Woodside and Birkenhead buses ran on their own services to Bromborough, Eastham, Thurstaston and Heswall, which we shall also look at in our photographs.

THE LANDSCAPE

The Wirral peninsula is like a stepping stone between the flat land on the other side of the Mersey and the great hills on the other side of the Dee. Although the south end of Wirral, outside Chester, is flat, a wooded ridge rises at Burton and runs for 10 miles along the Dee flank of the peninsula to West Kirby, with heathery heights and red sandstone outcrops at Burton, Heswall, Thurstaston and Caldy and a high point of 359 feet at Heswall Hill. Another ridge rises behind Bebington and runs 4½ miles along the Mersey flank to Bidston. This is the ridge behind Birkenhead: Storeton Hill (230 feet), Prenton Ridge (259 feet), Oxton Ridge (230 feet), Flaybrick Hill (175 feet) and Bidston Hill (238 feet).

The western ridge of Wirral runs about 1 mile inland from the Dee bank and the eastern ridge about 2 miles from the Mersey bank. Most of the towns and villages of Wirral are on the slopes between the ridges and the river banks and most of those are along the Mersey bank. The sylvan suburbs of Prenton, Oxton and Noctorum urbanised the top of the Merseyside ridge but the houses were so hidden among mature trees that the whole ridge appeared to be wooded.

Mid-Wirral is a gently undulating patchwork of pastureland, cornfields, coverts and woods. The rich green pastures of the Cheshire Cheese dairy herds are offset by the golden browns of wheat and barley fields as we get to the lighter soils and sunnier climes towards the coast, and this gave rise to the straw thatching tradition of the Wirral peninsula. The fields and lanes are bordered by trim hedgerows dotted with curly oak trees with fascinating tracery when picked out by winter sunlight and shadow. Many miles of road are bordered by red sandstone walls of farms, farmyards and gardens and covered by tunnels of trees. Pine trees are a feature of the hillsides and villa gardens.

Cheshire was also a black and white county: a land of black and white Friesian dairy cows grazing the pastures, black and white timber-framed inns on the roadside and neo-Tudor timbered villas behind the hedges and trees, black and white banded cast-iron signposts pointing out the villages and mileages, and black and white iron railings replacing hedges on the corners at road junctions to improve visibility – a feature that I think was unique to Cheshire.

SUBURBAN ENCROACHMENT

Across the cornfields between Raby and Willaston, before the eastern ridge obscures the sightline, you can see the tower of Liverpool Cathedral 7 miles away with no other building in the view. You would not imagine that you were so close to a large city. As you go north through the vale of mid-Wirral the suburbs close in from both sides but are still hidden by the ridges and woods until you reach Woodchurch Road.

In 1950 Prenton and Woodchurch were on the march towards each other, but the smokestack of the Co-op laundry struck an incongruous note in the still mainly rural scene. The small village of Woodchurch was entirely enclosed with its church and green within a wood till after the Second World War. In 1947 Birkenhead Corporation began building a housing estate on the east side of the village. The first houses were designed by Herbert Rowse (the Mersey Tunnel architect) in a cottage style around greens, and lay outside the wood, preserving the old village with its population of 129 in 1951. After 1952 the Borough

Architect, T. A. Brittain, took over and the estate expanded as a common council house estate and the old village was gradually swamped by the new. There was more unspoiled country between Woodchurch Road and Upton Road, but the rural idyll ended there.

The suburbanisation of Upton and Moreton began in the 1930s with houses and shopping parades sporting the Tudor gables, pebble-dash, pantiles and sun blinds characteristic of that period. However, the centre of Upton retained something of its village character. This was a market town till 1662 and retained a twice-yearly cattle fair till the mid-19th century. After the war Upton and Moreton continued to grow with more functional private and council housing estates. Moreton had lost its sandstone cottages and was entirely suburban in character; however, the centre was attractively laid out around the gardens of an irregular, elongated traffic island and was dominated by a large picturesque inn, the Coach and Horses, of 1927, a lively and elaborate composition of timber-framing and red sandstone in the Cheshire neo-Tudor revival style invoked by breweries in Liverpool and Wirral in the period when it was built, like the Boot Inn, Liscard. Its carved stone buttresses and doorways were so ecclesiastical that it was known as The Cathedral.

We crossed the borough boundary between Birkenhead and Wallasey as we dipped downhill halfway along the road from Upton, on its 100-foot knoll, to Moreton, on low-lying land that stretches along the Wirral coast west of Wallasey. The name Moreton means the farmstead or village by the mere, old English for a marsh or a lake, usually a reed-fringed lagoon. The land north of Moreton was salt marsh that was liable to flooding before the construction of Leasowe embankment, the damming of Wallasey Pool for docks and the drainage of the area by Wallasey Corporation. A period of heavy rain could flood all the low-lying land between Wallasey and Great Meols.

Wallasey did not have an attractive rural hinterland like Birkenhead. In 1928 the borough boundary was extended to take in Moreton and Leasowe, where a shanty town on stilts and wheels, with no sanitation or water supply, had grown up after the First World War on the meadows north of Moreton that were still prone to flooding.

Wallasey Corporation drained the land, laid sewers and water pipes and replaced the shacks and caravans with semi-detached council houses, and these estates were still being extended after the Second War. Leasowe was never a village, just a tract of marsh that became subtopia.

In 1933 the County Borough was extended again to Saughall Massie, a small rustic village of red sandstone cottages down a quiet country lane from the west end of Moreton with a population of 315 in 1951. It looked rather odd to see the relatively large, modern hotel in the centre of this small village and the double-deck Corporation buses that terminated outside. By the margin of a quarter of a mile of countryside this was the only rural bus terminus in the borough and Saughall Massie Hotel got free publicity as the destination on the blinds. The hotel replaced the old Saughall Arms of 1605.

Reeds Lane joins the amorphous, merging housing estates of Moreton and Leasowe and leads us to Leasowe Castle. This building is a multi-angular assemblage of castellated towers, gables and turrets in red sandstone and decorative timber framework. It was begun in 1593 as an octagonal tower, an outpost for the Stanleys, Earls of Derby, at a time of Protestant and Puritan persecution of Roman Catholics. It was considerably enlarged with residential wings for its 18th- and 19th-century gentry.

After the Civil War of 1642-45, when Cromwell ousted the Stanleys for their support of Charles I and suspended the races, the castle had a chequered history. It was, in turn, a ruin, a farmhouse, a stately home, a hospital for shipwrecked mariners, a hotel, a stately home again, a hotel again, a convalescent home, an army camp, a prisoner of war camp, and a convalescent home again from 1919 to 1971. (The changing fortunes of the castle since then are given under the picture on page 139.)

The low-lying coast at Leasowe is protected by a stone-faced embankment built in 1829-50, 2 miles long, sloping to the sea. This was the first stretch of the Wirral coast to be walled. It was erected by Liverpool Corporation, then the port authority, both to protect the low-lying land and to maintain the scour of Rock Channel as the (then) main approach to the port, marked by the lighthouses at Leasowe (1763) and Bidston (1771), both built by Liverpool. The scour of the Rock Channel into the

Mersey would be dissipated if the sea broke through the eroding dunes and spread across the fens to Wallasey Pool. In historic and recent times, even with the wall, storms with high spring tides or periods of heavy rain have flooded the coastal marshes. This was the area where in ancient times high tides flowed both ways between Moreton Shore and Wallasey Pool to make Wallasey an island. If nature had taken its course, Wallasey might still be an island today. Rock Channel was still used by Llandudno steamers, coasters, dredgers and fishing boats in the 1950s.

Liverpool began building the embankment a year after Thomas Telford mooted a ship canal from Dawpool (Thurstaston) to Wallasey Pool. He was engaged by William Laird, the Birkenhead shipbuilder, and Sir John Tobin, the Liscard land-owner, who were planning to build docks at Birkenhead and wanted back-door access to Wallasey Pool without paying hefty dues to Liverpool. Telford proposed a ship canal across Wirral with entrance locks at Dawpool. Ships would pay lower dues to the port of Chester by using a 5-mile dredged channel in the Dee estuary leading to Dawpool, beyond the port of Liverpool limits at Hilbre Point.

The canal was planned to pass south of Great Meols and between Moreton and Leasowe Lighthouse. There would then have been the strange spectacle of two lanes of ocean-going ships passing close to each other on both sides of the lighthouse and the embankment, with Rock Channel on one side and the ship canal on the other. The ship canal would again have made Wallasey virtually an island, with only a narrow isthmus between the canal and the sea wall linking it to the mainland.

Between Wallasey promenade and Leasowe embankment stretched the last half-mile of Cheshire's natural coastline: a range of sandhills linking the sea walls that embanked the remaining 7 miles between Rock Point, New Brighton, and Hilbre Point, Hoylake. Out here among these loose dunes we could imagine ourselves far away in the sandhills on the wild coast of Cumberland, Norfolk or the Outer Hebrides. To the north, across the bay, lay the dune coast of Lancashire to Formby Point, while to the west the serrated silhouette of Snowdonia spread along the horizon.

Below right The centre of **EASTHAM** village is a peaceful backwater, by-passed by the busy A41 New Chester Road. The old Chester road, now Eastham Village Road, passes through the village, curving left at this junction with Stanley Lane (right) with the cenotaph at the apex. Morning sunlight picks out the octagonal spire with its dormer-like broaches on St Mary's Church. Spire and tower are merged by the buttresses continuing the outline of the spire and the broaches make the transition from the octagon of the spire to the square of the tower. In coaching days, before the coming of the Birkenhead Railway in 1840, Eastham was a busy crossroads of stage lines to Chester, Birkenhead, the Eastham Ferry route to Liverpool and the Queen's Ferry route to Wales, and up to 20 coaches called here daily. Eastham Ferry plied from a landing place 1 mile down-river from the village from 1509 to 1929, first from a sandstone jetty at Job's Ferry, later from a short iron pier with a floating stage at the Eastham Ferry Hotel, which was a riverside resort with its woods and pleasure gardens. The inter-war by-pass with its shop parades and semi-detached houses has preserved the character of the old village while creating a suburban Eastham on the west side. Eastham was 4 miles beyond the Birkenhead borough boundary but in the 1950s Corporation buses from Woodside terminated in the village (route 40) and another route (44) ran through the village from New Ferry Depot to Eastham Ferry Hotel. The name Eastham is known in the maritime world for the Eastham entrance locks to the Manchester Ship Canal and for Eastham oil dock, officially Queen Elizabeth II Dock, opened in 1954, alongside the locks, with its own entrance lock from the river. Oil is piped from there to Stanlow refinery. *Commercial postcard*

Bottom right Once the site of a 10th-century monastery and a 17th-century market town on the Chester-Birkenhead road, by 1949, the date of this picture, **BROMBOROUGH** was an inter-war suburb of Birkenhead on a loop road, by-passed by the New Chester Road, within the Borough of Bebington with a belt of industry along the Mersey bank. The red sandstone cross in the old market place commemorates the site of the once weekly market with a charter dating from 1278. The ancient, weather-worn steps are all that survive of the old market cross, the ornate Victorian shaft being added in 1874. By the mid-20th century the few surviving 17th-century stone buildings and mid-Victorian merchants' villas were lost to view in a sea of semi-detached houses and parades of shops developed in the 1920s and '30s,

and the old market place was a stage on Birkenhead Corporation bus routes to Woodside, Eastham and Moreton and the terminus of routes to New Brighton and Overchurch.

On the right are W. Y. Hodgson's grocery shop and the Royal Oak Inn. In the background, on the corner of High Street (left) and Bromborough Village Road (right) are (from the left) Trufit (shoe shop), Sidney Samuel (photographer), Kay's (ladies' and children's outfitter), Kay's (draper and men's outfitter) and Alex Smith (funeral furnisher). Bromborough Pool Village, nearby, antedates Port Sunlight as a workers' garden suburb, having been created by Price's Patent Candle Company between 1853 and 1901 with a school, a chapel, two hospitals, a village hall, library, playing field, bowling green and allotments. The 142 terraced and semi-detached two- and three-bedroom houses were built in a cottage style not unlike those of Port Sunlight but more uniform and utilitarian in design and with the advantages of cavity walls, internal wc's and good back gardens. The old candle factory is now part of a chemical works. *Valentine's postcard*

Above left This was the former village street of **BEBINGTON** on the stage coach route from Parkgate to Tranmere and Woodside. The white building beyond the lollipop tree in the middle distance of this 1951 view is the Rose & Crown Inn of 1732, and small, ivy-covered, rustic terraced houses and shops enclosed the junction with Heath Road just over the brow. Otherwise Bebington had grown into a town of 1920s and '30s semi-detached houses with parades of modern shops on Church Road (behind the camera) and the centre of a Municipal Borough taking in Spital, Bromborough, Eastham, Storeton Brimstage, Thornton Hough and Raby. The building with the clock tower was the public library and museum, endowed by Joseph Mayer (1803-86), a Liverpool goldsmith and silversmith, who retired to Bebington at Pennant House. Mayer bought the neighbouring farm and laid out the land as a public park in 1869. He converted the farmhouse, of 1716, to a public library in 1870, adding the clock tower, and replaced the barn (beyond the clock tower) with the Mayer Hall art gallery and museum in 1878. The gateway on the extreme right of the picture is the entrance to Mayer Park. Pennant House, behind the library, became the Municipal Offices. In 1955 a start was made on building new municipal offices, civic hall and library on the left-hand side of the street, which was widened and transformed by the new buildings with their spacious, open landscaping, completed in the early 1970s – the final expression of the municipality of Bebington before local government re-organisation in 1974. *Valentine's postcard*

Left We are only 4 miles from Woodside Ferry, looking towards Birkenhead, and suburban Bebington lies just over the wooded ridge of Storeton Hill (230 feet) in the background. The dapper country gentleman looks slightly incongruous in this rustic setting, walking briskly along **BRIMSTAGE LANE** from Great Storeton to Brimstage in the forenoon of this fine mid-winter's day in 1962.

Above This 1950 photograph is of Telegraph Road, the centre of **HESWALL**, a small town on the A540 road from Chester to Hoylake, on heathery heights with views over the Dee estuary. The town centre at this point is 284 feet above the Dee and the road ascends to 340 feet at the north end of the town, where the water tower crowns Heswall Hill, 359 feet, the highest point in Wirral. Telegraph Road, a continuation of Chester High Road through Heswall and Thurstaston, is named after the former shipping telegraph station on Grange Hill above West Kirby.

The King's Picture House on the right opened in 1928 with 900 seats on one floor, having been upgraded from the old King's Hall of 1912, which was a combined public hall, church and cinema. The red sandstone building behind the trees on the left is Lloyd's Bank, built in 1904 on the corner of The Mount. Beyond, recessed behind a service road, are Castle Buildings, of 1936, with a parade of shops. The Mount (left at the signals) is a stone-walled lane winding downhill to the old village of Heswall, lying snugly halfway down the Deeside slope of Wirral with sporadic housing reaching to the shore. It takes some feat of map-reading to find Heswall's 200-yard Marine Drive on the river bank. In the 19th and 20th centuries the village extended uphill to the modern town on the main road along the top of the slope. Pensby Road (right at the signals) is an inter-war ribbon development of semi-detached houses and shops through Pensby to Thingwall on the way to Birkenhead. From 1930 Birkenhead Corporation buses ran out to Heswall via Thurstaston (route 71) or Irby (71A) and terminated in the Crosville bus station just this side of the picture house. In 1933 Heswall became the administrative centre of Wirral Urban District, extending to Gayton, Barnston, Irby and Thurstaston, although the district was still more rural than urban. The King's Picture House closed in 1958. *Valentine's postcard*

The hamlet of Landican lies in a quiet backwater half a mile down **LANDICAN LANE** from the A552 Woodchurch Road, and the lane continues as a cart track from Landican to Little Storeton, bordered by grass banks and stunted, curly oak trees amid the placid fields of mid-Wirral. This photograph is dated 1952 and Landican and its lane remain unchanged over the years, a peaceful enclave of rural Wirral with the spread of suburbia not far away. The lane is still used by horses if not by carts.

TOWNFIELD LANE led to Oxton over the ridge that hid Birkenhead from rural Wirral. St Saviour's parish church of 1891 stands on top of the ridge in this 1954 view and the village of Oxton, urbanised in Victorian times as part of Birkenhead, slopes down the other side of the ridge beyond the church. Oxton cricket and athletic grounds are beyond the wood on the right.

This typical Wirral landscape is the west side of Oxton Ridge (230 feet). The wood on the hilltop shrouds Noctorum, a suburb of high-class villas, mostly late-Victorian, entirely among the tall birches, larches and pines. We can just see the gables of the timber-framed house The Uplands peering over the hilltop in the middle of the picture and the red sandstone Mere Hall tucked in the edge of the wood on the right. The population of Noctorum declined from 212 in 1901 to 192 in 1951. This 1954 view is taken from South Road, a cart track running across the picture from upper left to lower right.

Emerging from Noctorum wood, the wide, stony cart track of **SOUTH ROAD** led south along the west side of Oxton Ridge. In 1954 two ladies are sitting on a bench seat with a view west over the cornfields in the vale of mid-Wirral to the wooded ridges of west Wirral and the mountains of north Wales beyond.

South Road led south from Noctorum to Prenton. In this 1954 view south through the wide vale of mid-Wirral we can see smoke rising from the chimney stack of the Co-op laundry on Woodchurch Road and the outliers of the Birkenhead Corporation housing estate at Woodchurch, begun in 1946.

The village of **WOODCHURCH** was just that – a church in a wood. The village was entirely enclosed in a wood, like Noctorum, with cottages clustered among the trees around the churchyard. William Bennett's White Cottage, once the village Post Office, was tucked into the stone wall and the hedge in Pool Lane as it entered the village from Arrowe Park Road. The red sandstone parish church of the Holy Cross dates from the 12th century. The 14th-century tower, seen over the roof of the cottage in this 1954 photograph, was rebuilt in the 16th century with massive stepped buttresses that give it style as well as support.

Below From **POOL LANE, WOODCHURCH**, we look
north-east to Bidston Hill (238 feet), 2 miles away across
country, again in 1954. The wooded ridge hid Birkenhead from
its rural hinterland and formed the backdrop to the town when
viewed from the Mersey. Telegraph poles were a common sight
alongside country roads, carrying overhead telephone lines,
later ducted underground.

Bottom   From the 300-foot-high, red-rock plateau of
THURSTASTON HILL we get this view west across the Dee
estuary, 5 miles wide at the mouth, to the north coast of Wales.
This is the largest out-thrust of bare red sandstone in Wirral and
the A540 Chester-Hoylake road dives through the western edge
of the hill in a dramatic cutting between sheer cliffs of red rock.

The hill is surrounded by the heathery slopes of Thurstaston
Heath. More than 140 acres of rock and heath are preserved as
a public open space; Birkenhead Corporation pioneered this
philanthropy by buying the 50 acres of rock hilltop in 1881,
although it was then more than 4 miles beyond the borough
boundary. The remaining 90 acres of heath were donated by the
land-owners to the National Trust in 1916-17. Birkenhead
Corporation buses ran out to Thurstaston from 1930. The
village of Caldy can be seen in the distance on the right.
Commercial postcard

Right As seen here at **THURSTASTON SHORE** in 1960,
cliffs of boulder clay up to 60 feet high stretch along the Dee
bank of Wirral from Heswall to Caldy. At Thurstaston a lane

led to the station, two-thirds of a mile
from the village, on the Hooton-West
Kirby railway, which closed in 1956. At
the end of Station Road, a footpath
cascades down the cliffs, clothed with
hawthorn bushes, to these lonely
cottages on the shore, built circa 1850 as
a coastguard station. They are known as
Shore Cottages, also as Sally's Cottage
(after Sally McCrae, who died in 1953)
and are marked on some maps as
Dawpool Cottages. There are other
Dawpool Cottages on the western edge
of Thurstaston Heath and a Dawpool
Farm at Thurstaston, while Dawpool
Hall between the heath and the village
was the home of Thomas Ismay, founder
of the White Star Line in 1869. Dawpool
was one of the dependant anchorages of

the port of Chester. There are records of the Dublin packet landing at Dawpool in the 18th century and the shore is strewn with stone blocks that might be from a ruined quay or jetty. In 1822 there was a proposal to establish 'a dock and a line of steamers at Dawpool' and in 1828 Thomas Telford proposed a ship canal across north Wirral to Wallasey Pool with entrance locks at Dawpool, approached by a 5-mile dredged channel in the Dee estuary, but these schemes foundered along with other ambitious dreams of 19th-century engineers and entrepreneurs. In the 1950s Birkenhead Corporation buses ran from Woodside to Thurstaston Shore (route 74) at summer weekends. Beyond Shore Cottages we see the cliffs stretching away to Caldy golf links.

Below **ARROWE** is a hamlet of plain, terraced houses on the A551 Arrowe Park Road between Woodchurch and Upton. In 1951 a mother and two children are waiting at the bus stop (left), a cyclist heads along the country road to Upton, and a 1948 Austin lorry is carrying crates of vegetables. Arrowe House Farm was on the far corner of Arrowe Brook Road (left) and the railing and stone wall on the near corner mark the beginning of Arrowe Park, the 425-acre grounds of Arrowe Hall, bought in 1927 by Birkenhead Corporation as a public park. Arrowe Park was the site of the 1929 World Scout Jamboree to mark the 21st anniversary of the Boy Scout movement, which the Chief Scout, Lt Gen Sir Robert Baden-Powell, founded in Birkenhead in 1908.

Above Two and a quarter miles from the town centre of Birkenhead, the road to Upton was up in the country and fresh air on top of **FLAYBRICK HILL**, 175 feet above the Mersey, among the pines, birches and heather that cover the sandstone ridge forming the divide between Birkenhead and its rural hinterland. This 1954 view is looking west from Boundary Road crossing, and here the concrete lamp posts of town gave way to the cast-iron lamp posts that continued along the rural reaches of the A5027 road. Boundary Road was the borough boundary before Birkenhead extended the county borough to Woodchurch and Upton in 1933.

Left A 1948 Wallasey Corporation bus descends Upton Road on the west side of **BIDSTON HILL** on route 18 from New Brighton to Arrowe Park, Woodchurch, via Upton in 1954. This joint service with Birkenhead Corporation was the only real escape route into the country for Wallasey bus drivers apart from the short rural section to Saughall Massie, whereas Birkenhead buses also ran out to Eastham, Heswall and Thurstaston.

Above With its flower beds and oil lamps, **UPTON STATION** was the first rustic stop on the train journey from Seacombe to Wrexham. The line runs north-south alongside the Fender Brook through the vale of mid-Wirral between Bidston Hill and the rise that gave its name to Upton. There was a small inter-war housing estate called Ford on the east (left) side of the station, which is three-quarters of a mile from the centre of Upton. This 1951 photograph is taken from the top of the steps from the booking office on the A5027 road bridge, looking south to the post-war housing estate at Woodchurch and the chimney of the Co-op laundry. Upton station opened in 1896 to a standard design of the North Wales & Liverpool Railway, an arm of the Great Central, which officially took over the line in 1905, giving running powers to

Cheshire Lines goods trains. It became an isolated enclave of the far-reaching LNER empire from the grouping in 1923, and thus part of the LNER and Cheshire Lines freight route to Birkenhead docks and their dockland depots at Woodside, Poulton and Seacombe. On nationalisation in 1948 the line became part of the Midland Region of British Railways.

Below This view of **FORD ROAD, UPTON**, the main street of the village, shows St Mary's Church and the Eagle & Crown Hotel on the corner of Rake Lane (right). Ford Road leads down to Upton station and over Bidston Hill to Birkenhead. The shops on the left were Charles Gainer (baker), Leonard's (fruiterer), Thomas Heseltine (butcher), Jones (baker) and Hilda Owens (hairdresser). *F. Frith postcard © The Francis Frith Collection*

Above **ALL HILL COTTAGE** was the name of this former tollhouse on the corner of Greasby Road (left) and Saughall Massie Road (right) at Upton. The 'windows' facing the camera are painted on the blank wall. In the distance in 1954 we can see the village of Greasby, pronounced 'Grayzbee' by the old Cheshire people before it became a suburb of Liverpool; it was spelt Gravesby in 1150 and Graysby in 1611.

Below **STEAM TAR SPRAYING, GREASBY**. The steam lorry was still a common sight on Merseyside in the mid-20th century, used mainly by millers and sugar refiners and for tar spraying on roadworks. The grim countenance of the Sentinel undertype steam lorry, with a vertical boiler and chimney at the front of the cab, the steam engine under the chassis and chain drive with two giant bicycle chains to the back wheels, a design dating from 1911, was the general type still in use after the Second World War. The Sentinel Waggon Works, of Shrewsbury, went on building steam lorries until 1950 and maintained a service depot at Duke's Dock, Liverpool, until 1957 (when the company was sold to Rolls-Royce) because of the number of these vehicles in dockland, where they continued working until 1962. Twelve ex-Liverpool steam lorries survive in preservation today.

This example is a Sentinel DG4P, a double-geared four-wheeler on pneumatic tyres. The driver had to stop to change gear, but the lower gear was used only on steep hills and rough ground. It was built in 1929 as a flatbed lorry for A. E. Knox of Erdington, Birmingham, for brick haulage and was sold in 1942 to Dee, Cestrian & Laycock (mineral waters) of Chester. Robert Bridson & Son, contractors, of Neston, bought it in 1944 and converted it to a tar sprayer by mounting a tar boiler on the flat platform, heated by steam from the boiler in the cab. A small steam pump, spray bar and hand lance were fitted at the back. It is pictured tar spraying on Frankby Road, Greasby, in 1954 and continued working on Wirral roads until 1968. It was sold second-hand to Lloyd-Jones brothers of Ruthin and went on tar spraying in Denbighshire from 1968 until 1984, when it was the last steam road locomotive in commercial use. It languished till 1997, when it was sold for preservation. Its present owner, David Hilditch of Middletown, near Welshpool, has restored it to full working order as a tar sprayer in the livery and lettering of Lloyd-Jones brothers.

Above right Descendants of the silver birches that once covered Birkenhead still grow on the slopes of the wooded **BIDSTON HILL**, which forms the backdrop to the town, seen here in 1972. The ground here is a patchwork of bare rock, grass and heather. Ferns, firs, pines, gorse and rhododendrons also clothe the hillsides, and the 238-foot summit is paved in bare red sandstone, eroded into flat slabs. The hill is dotted with large villas, but Birkenhead Corporation saved it from further development by buying 90 acres of the summit between 1894 and 1908 as a public recreational open space – long before the borough boundary was extended over the hill in 1933.

Below The disused but preserved tower windmill with sails that crowns the summit of Bidston Hill was built in 1791 to replace a 1596 post mill wrecked in a gale. Despite storm damage in 1821 and again in 1834, it carried on milling by windpower till 1864. The mill was bought for preservation by Birkenhead Corporation in 1894 together with the authority's first 47 acres of public open space on Bidston Hill. All the Wirral windmills had their sails luffed into the wind by a large pulley wheel, like this one, instead of a fantail, at the back of the cap. The wheel turned a pinion against a rack around the top of the tower and the miller luffed the sails by turning the wheel with an endless chain from the ground. This postcard view is dated 1935. *Valentine's postcard*

Above **BIDSTON OBSERVATORY** – the Liverpool Observatory & Tidal Institute – on the north end of the summit ridge of Bidston Hill, gave the official tide predictions for two-thirds of the world from the 1920s to the 1950s. It was built in 1866-67 from the rock excavated for the foundations and cellars when the Mersey Docks & Harbour Board moved its Liverpool Observatory from Waterloo Dock to Bidston Hill. Its functions were to determine the exact longitude of Liverpool and exact time by observing the stars from the transit telescope in the east dome, to test and rate ships' chronometers against the stars, and to record the weather and issue local weather forecasts for shipping. An equatorial telescope in the west dome observed comets. The boom of the One O'clock Gun at Morpeth Dock was operated by remote control from Bidston Observatory for ships to set their chronometers, used for determining longitude at sea.

The University of Liverpool Tidal Institute installed tide-predicting machines here in 1924, 1929 and 1949. These mechanical computers could calculate the heights and times of tides for every coast and creek on earth at any time in the future or past. The tide tables for British waters, ports of the British Empire and many foreign countries were based on these calculations made on Bidston Hill. During the Second World War Bidston Observatory prepared the tidal predictions for operations in Burma, Holland and Normandy. And when the tide flowed up the Mersey the increasing weight of water on the Birkenhead bank was felt by seismographs in the cellars, which could measure earth tremors anywhere in the world. From 1961 the observatory changed its name four times as it came under the aegis of a succession of institutions that concentrated oceanographic work at Bidston and spread to a new building alongside in 1975. Weather records from 1867 ended in 2002 and the observatory closed as the oceanographic laboratory moved to Liverpool University in 2003. The 1949 tide-predicting machine and the transit telescope are now in Liverpool Museum. On the north side of the observatory, facing over Bidston Moss to the sea, is a lighthouse, which was erected for Liverpool shipping in 1771, rebuilt in 1872-73 and shut down in 1913 after Rock Channel had been marked by flashing buoys. *Commercial postcard*

Right Below the northern promontory of Bidston Hill, the red sandstone village of **BIDSTON** nestles on the lower slopes. The streets of Birkenhead ended abruptly a quarter of a mile short of Bidston to give the village a protective green belt, and the A553 road from Birkenhead wound round the hill and through the village on its way to Moreton and Hoylake. On the right of this 1954 view is St Oswald's Church with its early-16th-century tower and its mid-19th-century nave. The cottage beyond the churchyard at 1 School Lane was the Ring O' Bells public house from circa 1750 to 1868. On the left is part of the 17th-century farmhouse of Church Farm, followed by its early-18th-century barn on the next bend in the road, where the village ended.

Below right In 1952 an LMS electric train of 1938 stock is drawn up at the Liverpool-bound face of the island platform at **BIDSTON STATION**, a remote junction with wooden station buildings and signal cabin at the end of School Lane, Bidston. The station was on the edge of Bidston Golf Links on the fens of Bidston Moss, which in ancient times were salt marshes over which high tides flowed to isolate Wallasey, and the line can be seen heading west across the fens towards Leasowe and Moreton on the horizon.

The railway between Birkenhead and Hoylake opened in 1866 and Bidston East Junction was the hub of the Wirral Railway system, which in 1891 amalgamated lines laid by pioneer companies from Birkenhead Park to West Kirby with branches to New Brighton and Seacombe. Bidston was also the junction with the Great Central route to Wrexham, which opened in 1896 and forks off to the left at Dee Junction by the signals at the far end of the station. This bleak junction was the end of the GCR line, but that company's trains continued to Seacombe and to dockland good stations under running powers. Trains from Wrexham crossed the West Kirby line here and used the Wirral Railway branch to Seacombe under running powers from 1896.

In 1923 the GCR became part of the LNER and the Wirral Railway became part of the LMS. In 1938 the LMS electrified the lines to West Kirby and New Brighton with a live third rail and through running over the Mersey Railway from Birkenhead Park to Liverpool. Trains call at Bidston station on the way from Liverpool to West Kirby but New Brighton trains only pass through Bidston East Junction. Wrexham trains were diverted to New Brighton when the Seacombe branch closed in 1960 and have terminated at Bidston since 1978. The GCR thrust into Wirral was aimed at Birkenhead docks. To the south (left) of Bidston station GCR/LNER lines led through extensive goods sidings at Bidston East Junction and alongside Beaufort Road to Shore Road goods depot at Woodside. The Seacombe branch gave access to the Wallasey dock road and goods depots at Poulton and Seacombe.

Above The County Borough of Wallasey was extended to take in **SAUGHALL MASSIE** in 1933. This small village was in the south-west corner of the borough in open country, only a quarter of a mile beyond the reach of suburban Upton and Moreton. The suffix Massey was a reference to the lords of the manor of Bidston, the de Mascy family from Massy in France. Saughall Road is lined with red sandstone walls and hedges and there are red sandstone cottages to left and right. The thatched Ivy Cottage on the right of this 1954 photograph is dated 1666. The Saughall Massie Hotel, which stands prominently in the centre of the village, was the terminus of Wallasey Corporation bus route 4, from Seacombe via Pasture Road, the only rural bus terminus in the borough.

Below This is the view south along **UPTON ROAD, MORETON**, the country road between the two villages, in 1954. We crossed the borough boundary from Wallasey to Birkenhead at the line of trees on the left at the foot of Upton Knoll (100 feet), where the road began to climb between sandstone walls through a tunnel of trees into Upton village.

The former parish church of Upton was remotely sited at Overchurch and the remains of its burial ground lay among the trees to the right. The church, of Saxon foundation, was pulled down in 1813, a new church was built in Upton, and a runic monument to one Æthelmund is now in Chester Museum. A small housing estate inheriting the name of Overchurch lay between the site of the church and the village of Saughall Massie. The woman on the left, with headscarf, long overcoat and leather shopping bag, is on her way to the bus stop and Birkenhead (route 77).

Top right **HOYLAKE ROAD, MORETON**, was the main road through the village on the way from Birkenhead to Hoylake. We are looking west at Moreton Cross, where an elongated floral island regulates traffic at the central crossroads. Most of the shops are along the north-south axis leading to Leasowe and Upton. Here in 1953 we see Moreton's two main hostelries, the Plough Inn (right), built in 1931, and the large red sandstone and timber-framed Coach & Horses beyond the roundabout, built in 1927. Both replaced earlier inns. The former village of Moreton became a suburb of Wallasey in 1928, when the county borough boundary was extended to take in Moreton and Leasowe and bring drainage and sanitation to the rural slums, shanties and caravans on these

meadows and marshes. At the same time Wallasey renamed Birkenhead Road, east of Moreton Cross, to avoid confusion with Birkenhead Road, Seacombe, and the main road became Hoylake Road right through Moreton. The 1948 Wallasey bus is on route 5 from Bermuda Road, Moreton, to Seacombe Ferry via Reeds Lane and Leasowe Castle. *Valentine's postcard*

Above right **LEASOWE CASTLE** has a history as chequered as its architecture might imply. It was a Railwaymen's Convalescent Home from 1911 till 1971, except when it housed prisoners during the First World War. It began in 1595 as an octagonal tower for the Stanleys, Earls of Derby, and was extended in the early 17th century with four square, gabled towers on alternate angles of the octagon. As Royalists in the Civil War, the Stanleys lost their estates and the castle fell into ruin. Thus it was marked on 17th- and 18th-century maps as Mockbeggar Hall and gave its name to the shore, which is still marked Mockbeggar Wharf on maps today. Towards the end of the 17th century the hall became a farmhouse. Its most illustrious period was from 1778 to 1895, when it was much enlarged as a stately home for successive families of Cheshire gentry. Mrs Margaret Boode, widow of a West Indian planter,

lived there from 1802, and in 1818 she employed John Foster of Liverpool to design alterations, extensions and much of the frontage we see today. She used part of the building as a hospital for mariners shipwrecked on Leasowe shore. The most notable resident was her son-in-law, General the Hon Sir Edward Cust, Bart, KCH MP MC to Queen Victoria, decorated by the King of Belgium and the Emperor of Austria, senior magistrate for Wirral and author of military history and scripture books. He owned the castle from 1826 to 1878, used it as a hotel from 1828 to 1848, then as a residence till he died in 1878. Sir Edward lined his dining room with panelling from the Star Chamber of Westminster with its starry ceiling, fitted his library with oak from the submerged forest on the Wirral coast and enclosed the grounds with walls, gates and a gatehouse. His son, Sir Charles Cust, sold the castle in 1895 and it reverted to a hotel for the next 10 years. After 56 years as a convalescent home (excluding the four years as a prisoner of war camp), it was empty for three years, sold to the borough council in 1974 for an archive store and re-opened in 1980 as a hotel for the third time in its history. Leasowe Castle Hotel is not to be confused with the tavern of the same name in Seacombe. *F. Frith postcard, by permission of The Francis Frith Collection*

Above **LEASOWE SANDHILLS**, the stretch of loose dunes between Telegraph Lane and Leasowe Castle, was the last half-mile of the Cheshire coast left in its natural state between the sea walls that embanked the remaining 7 miles of coast between Rock Point, New Brighton, and Hilbre Point, Hoylake. In 1954 two ladies' bicycles with baskets prop each other up on the shore and a rug and picnic lay nearby as their owners dry themselves after a swim and change into their clothes at the top of the dunes.

Below In 1954 the stark bulk of the disused Leasowe Lighthouse passes its last years on the desolation of **LEASOWE COMMON**, surrounded by meres, rushes, tents, caravans and the cottages of the few hardy dwellers on the fens bordering the Wirral coast. The lighthouse was built in 1763, originally with a coal-fire beacon. Bales of Liverpool-bound cotton from a shipwreck were used to stabilise the foundations in the marshy ground for this seven-floor building rising 101 feet. The light went out in 1908 when Rock Channel was marked with flashing buoys. The lighthouse keepers for the last 14 years, Mrs Mary Williams and her daughter, kept the lighthouse open as a café until 1935. The mere in the foreground was one of several dug by First World War German prisoners from Leasowe Castle to drain Leasowe Common, which was used as a play area and a site for camping and circuses. The photograph was taken from the Leasowe embankment, the first stretch of the Wirral coast to be walled. The 2-mile embankment was built in 1829-50 to maintain the scour of the Rock Channel into Liverpool as much as to protect the low-lying coastal meadows. The coast had eroded 100 yards in 20 years before the wall was built and the sea threatened to break through the dunes. After a letter from Sir Edward Cust of Leasowe Castle in 1828, Liverpool Corporation, then the port authority, set up the Wallasey Embankment Commissioners to build the wall and levy rates in equal shares on the port and on the land-owners of the 5,828 acres below spring tide level; some of the marshes lay more than 6 feet below this level.

'Old boats low-moored upon the channel's edge
Asleep and dreaming of tomorrow's tide.'

These two lines of verse by the late John Pride, the Wirral poet and penman, about Parkgate, describe this low tide scene in the Dee estuary from Thurstaston shore in 1950. The fishing-boats moored along the channel's edge were the last vessels to use the forgotten, 18th-century landing place called Dawpool. This was the place where, in 1828, the civil engineer Thomas Telford proposed entrance locks to a ship canal across Wirral to Wallasey Pool and docks at Birkenhead. *The late George Greenwood*

BIBLIOGRAPHY

The following is a list of publications from which I have gleaned and sifted information. All but Gore's and Kelly's Directories are in my own library at home.

A.B.C. of Motorcar Spotting (1949) by Graeme L. Greenwood

Almost an Island: the story of Wallasey (1990) by Noel E. Smith

Around Wallasey and New Brighton (The Archive Photographs series, 1996) by Ralph Rimmer

An Atlas of Anglo-Saxon England (1981) by David Hill

Bygone Liverpool (1913) by Ramsay Muir

Canadian Pacific Afloat, 1883-1968 (1968) by George Musk

Canadian Pacific (1981) by George Musk

A Century of Local Government (1935) by Wallasey Corporation

Cheshire ('The Buildings of England' series, 1971) by Nikolaus Pevsner and Edward Hubbard

Cheshire ('The King's England' series, 1938) by Arthur Mee

The City of Liverpool Official Handbook (1950)County Borough of Wallasey Civic Week Handbook (1948)

Crosville Official Time Table (1949-50)

A Detailed History of the Wallasey Corporation Motor Bus Undertaking, 1929-1969 (unpublished, 1997) by T. B. Maund

Gore's Directory and View of Liverpool and Environs (1832 et seq)

The Guinness Book of Records (1956)

The History of Liverpool (1907) by Louis Lacey

An Introduction to Anglo-Saxon England (1970) by Peter Hunter Blair

The Inviting Shore: A Social History of New Brighton, 1830-1939 (1996) by Anthony M. Miller

Kelly's Directory of Liverpool, Including Bootle, Birkenhead, Wallasey and Environs (1950s and '60s)

The Liners of Liverpool, Parts I, II and III (1986-88) by Derek M. Whale

Liverpool (1920) by Ward, Lock & Company

Liverpool, City of Architecture (1999) by Quentin Hughes

Liverpool Colonnade (1955) by Richard Whittington-Egan

Liverpool Parish Church (1957) by members of the church

Liverpool's Railways (1998) by Paul Anderson

Liverpool Tramways, 1943 to 1957 by R. E. Blackburn

Local Transport in Wallasey (1969) by T. B. Maund

Lutyens (1981) by the Arts Council of Great Britain

The Mersey Estuary (1949) by J. E. Allison

Merseyside and District Railway Stations (1994) by Paul Bolger

The Observer's Book of Ships (1952) by Frank E. Dodman

The Old Mansions of Wallasey (1994) by J. S. Rebecca

Old Ordnance Survey Maps by Alan Godfrey

A Perambulation of the Hundred of Wirral (1909) by Harold Edgar Young

The Pictorial History of Liverpool Cathedral (1962) by the Dean, the Very Rev F. W. Dillistone

Popular Cars Illustrated (1949) by the Raleigh Press

Rails to Port and Starboard (Mersey dockside railways) (1992) by John W. Gahan

The Rise and Progress of Wallasey (1974) by E. C. Woods and P. C. Brown

The Railway Heritage of Britain (1983) by Gordon Biddle and O. S. Nock

Reflections on a River (1995) by Paul Boot and Nigel Bowker

The Romance of Wirral (1949) by Alice Caton

Seaport: Architecture and Townscape in Liverpool (1964) by Quentin Hughes

Seaside Piers (1977) by Simon H. Adamson

Ships of the Isle Of Man Steam Packet Company Ltd (1967) by Fred Henry

Ships of the Mersey and Manchester (1959) by H. M. Le Fleming

Ships of the Seven Seas, Nos 1 and 2 (1947 and 1948) by Charles Graham

Seventeen Stations to Dingle (1982) by John W. Gahan

The Silver Screens of Wirral (1989) by P. A. Carson and C. R. Garner

The Survey Gazetteer of the British Isles (1951) by John Bartholomew

A Topographical Dictionary of England (1848) by Samuel Lewis

The Tramways of Birkenhead and Wallasey (1987) by T. B. Maund and Martin Jenkins

Wallasey Corporation Motor Buses Time Tables (1950-51)

Wallasey of Yesteryear (1980) by Carol E. Bidston

Wallasey Old and New (1949) by the Wallasey News

Whitbread Book of Scouseology, Vol Two Merseyside Life 1900-1987 by Phil Young and Jim Bellew

The Wirral Peninsula (1955) by Norman Ellison

Yesterday's Wirral, No 4 Wallasey and New Brighton (1986) by Ian and Marylin Boumphrey
 No 5 Wallasey, New Brighton & Moreton (1988) by Ian and Marylin Boumphrey

Yesterday's Wirral Pictorial History, 1890 to 1953 (2000) by Ian and Marylin Boumphrey

INDEX

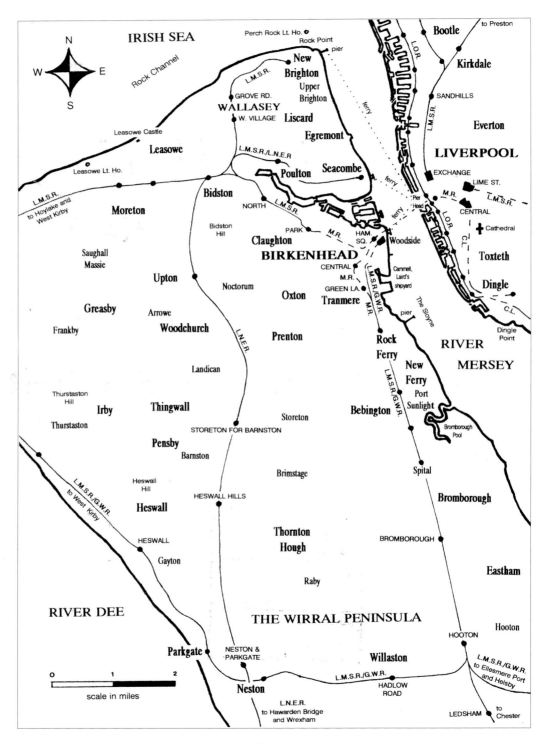

Map showing most of the places mentioned in the text of the two volumes, including the docks, piers, landing stages, railways and passenger stations. Broken lines are railway tunnels. Not shown are freight-only lines to the docks and industrial sites, or Liverpool Riverside station, which was just north of Pier Head, between Prince's Dock and the landing stage.